Teaching and Supporting Adult Learners

FURTHER EDUCATION

You might also like the following books from Critical Publishing

A Complete Guide to the Level 4 Certificate in Education and Training
By Lynn Machin, Duncan Hindmarch, Sandra Murray and Tina Richardson
978-1-909330-89-4 Published September 2013

A Complete Guide to the Level 5 Diploma in Education and Training
By Lynn Machin, Duncan Hindmarch, Sandra Murray and Tina Richardson
978-1-909682-53-5 September 2014

The A–Z Guide to Working in Further Education
By Jonathan Gravells and Susan Wallace
978-1-909330-85-6 Published September 2013

Dial M for Mentor: Critical reflections on mentoring for coaches, educators and trainers
By Jonathan Gravells and Susan Wallace
978-1-909330-00-9 Published September 2012

Equality and Diversity in Further Education
By Sheine Peart
978-1-909330-97-9 Published May 2014

Inclusion in Further Education
By Lydia Spenceley
978-1-909682-05-4 Published June 2014

The Professional Teacher in Further Education
By Keith Appleyard and Nancy Appleyard
978-1-909682-01-6 Published June 2014

Understanding the Further Education Sector: A Critical Guide to Policies and Practices
By Susan Wallace
978-1-909330-21-4 Published September 2013

Most of our titles are also available in a range of electronic formats. To order please go to our website www.criticalpublishing.com or contact our distributor, NBN International, 10 Thornbury Road, Plymouth PL6 7PP, telephone 01752 202301 or e-mail orders@nbninternational.com.

Teaching and Supporting Adult Learners

Jackie Scruton and Belinda Ferguson
Series Editor Susan Wallace

FURTHER EDUCATION

First published in 2014 by Critical Publishing Ltd

British Library Cataloguing in Publication Data
A CIP record for this book is available from the British Library

ISBN: 978-1-909682-13-9

This book is also available in the following e-book formats:

MOBI ISBN: 978-1-909682-14-6
EPUB ISBN: 978-1-909682-15-3
Adobe ebook ISBN: 978-1-909682-16-0

Cover and text design by Greensplash Limited
Project Management by Out of House Publishing
Printed and bound in Great Britain by Bell and Bain, Glasgow

Critical Publishing
152 Chester Road
Northwich
CW8 4AL
www.criticalpublishing.com

Contents

Acknowledgements

The Authors would like to acknowledge the registered trademarks that have been used within this text: Facebook, LinkedIn, Makaton, Friends Reunited, Microsoft, Skype, Moodle (with apologies if any have not been mentioned).

Many thanks to:

Sue Wallace: for her encouragement, guidance and for being there when the going was tough.

All our Learners: who over have over the years helped us to understand their needs.

Jackie would like to especially thank her husband John who has had to listen to endless conversations and read many drafts.

Belinda would like to thank her son James for his understanding and patience during this project.

Meet the authors

Jackie Scruton

I am a Senior Lecturer at Nottingham Trent University, and part of my role is to support adult learners on a range of undergraduate and postgraduate courses. I have taught adult learners in a range of settings and on courses, such as basic skills and degree programmes. I have a particular interest in working with learners for whom inclusion may be an issue, including adult learners. This interest was developed as a result of not only working with such learners but also my experience of 'finding' education later in life.

Belinda Ferguson

I am a Senior Lecturer in Education at Nottingham Trent University, currently teaching on part-time degrees and teacher training courses, previously having taught in FE for ten years on professional courses and initial teacher training. I have worked with adult learners throughout my career, and have seen the challenges and pressures they face along with the pleasure of success and the opportunities created. As a former mature postgraduate student I have empathy for students who find themselves juggling childcare and work with their studies.

Meet the series editor

Susan Wallace

I am Emeritus Professor of Education at Nottingham Trent University where, for many years, part of my role was to support learning on the initial training courses for teachers in the FE sector. I taught in the sector myself for ten years, including on BTEC programmes and basic skills provision. My particular interest is in the motivation and behaviour of students in Further Education, and in mentoring and the ways in which a successful mentoring relationship can support personal and professional development. I have written a range of books, mainly aimed at teachers and student teachers in the sector, and I enjoy hearing readers' own stories of FE, whether it's by e-mail or at speaking engagements and conferences.

Introduction

The aims of this book

This book has been written for teachers who want to develop their skills and knowledge in supporting adult learners. It is designed to help you create an inclusive approach to teaching and to enhance the experiences that you and your learners have.

By the end of this book you will be able to:

*   understand the policies impacting on post-compulsory education and training and the diversity of adult learners that participate in this sector;

*   recognise what motivates adult learners, the barriers they may face and how these impact on engagement with their learning;

*   analyse how adults learn and the importance of preparation to ensure an inclusive and structured learning approach;

*   ensure that the use of technology supports adult learners and enhances their learning experience;

*   analyse the importance of developing a collegiate approach when teaching and supporting adult learners;

*   critically analyse common teaching situations in order to improve practice.

The teaching of adult learners brings with it its own challenges and rewards. This is borne out by the authors' experiences of studying as mature, part-time learners themselves, and their experience (as teachers) of supporting countless students who have also studied this way. We want to share our experiences both as practitioners and as learners. In doing so, we aim to help you explore some of the theoretical concepts and practical strategies that might help your learners in their learning journey.

This book is the result of informal conversations over a number of years. They were the kind of conversations you probably have all the time in the office or the staffroom and often went something like this.

Jackie: *You know Tim; I've just had a long e-mail from him. He is struggling to write his assignment. He says he can't find many books or much information on his topic and those books he has are all old. He doesn't know where to start or how to structure his work; he thinks he may have chosen the wrong topic. His two-year-old daughter is ill and he is having to look after her and he is wondering whether he should keep coming to the sessions as it is a struggle or whether he should just give up and leave the course.*

Belinda: *Sounds familiar; like he's having a mid-course wobble. I have had a few of my group saying similar things. It's frustrating as we've talked through a lot of the issues that are raised and the information is available to them if they come and chat with us, and of course in the virtual learning environment.*

Jackie: *Yes I know, we think we've got it right, but maybe we need to think about other things or the same things in a different way. Remember when we …*

Belinda: *Yes, great and what about …*

Jackie: *Yes, and maybe we could try …*

Examples like this often help to develop our knowledge and practice, support our adult learners and give us the confidence to realise we can do it. We firmly believe the saying *you are never too old to learn* and we anticipate continuing to do this, not only through our own formal study but also from the wealth of knowledge and experience that the adults we teach bring to the classroom. We can all learn from each other, and we hope you can inspire your learners as we have been inspired by the teachers we've met along the way.

When we started to plan what to write about in this book, we discovered that there were a number of published texts (for example, Rogers and Horrocks, 2010, Gray et al., 2000 and Gravells and Simpson, 2012) which explore the themes of teaching adult learners. However, most of these texts focus on teaching adult learners within the Further Education (FE) context. In this book we explore this area but also discuss in more generic terms the needs of adult learners within broader educational contexts across adult, higher and Further Education and training. We don't explore specific types of educational establishments, but rather the need all adult learners might have for 'different' types of support. For example, they often have busy lives and encounter difficulties with time management or other personal challenges. The strategies you use as a teacher to engage and support your adult learners will apply whatever the sector, level or type of provision.

This book is aimed at trainees and teachers who work in a range of educational institutions, teaching on a diversity of courses. We hope that it enables you to develop your understanding in order to create effective teaching strategies which meet the needs of your adult learners.

Who are adult learners and what do we mean by adult education?

When reading about working with adult learners you may well come across the term 'andragogy'. The word defines a philosophy and way of teaching and working specifically with adult learners, implying that a specific skill set is required. This skill set is arguably different from the one we need when teaching children, which we refer to as 'pedagogy'. The specialised concept of andragogy was developed primarily by Knowles et al. (1984). They argued that there were five characteristics that define an adult learner.

1. **Self concept**: as a child matures into adulthood their self concept changes from being dependent to being self-directed. We give you examples of this in Chapter 3, where you can read a number of different students' stories.

2. **Experience**: this clearly comes with age and enables the learner to use their own experiences in their learning. You can read about an example of this in Ben's story in Chapter 2.

3. **Readiness to learn**: as a child matures into adulthood the readiness to learn is linked to the development of their role within society. We explore this further in Chapter 4.

4. **Orientation to learn**: learning in childhood can often take the form of learning knowledge, but without much thought about how that might be applied. As the child matures this changes to become application of knowledge to 'problem solving'.

5. **Motivation to learn**: internal motivation develops as learners grow and mature. We discuss this in greater detail in Chapter 3.

As you read this book and engage with the critical thinking activities and student/tutor stories (in Chapter 2), you are encouraged to reflect on how these characteristics may apply to your own adult learners and what they imply in terms of good practice for you as a teacher and supporter of learning.

It is important at this stage that we define the term 'adult learner'. The following examples provide a range of working definitions.

*   Firstly Wlodkowski (1999) suggests that they are people who are responsible for their life and who have some social responsibility. They will be financially independent and either in paid employment or voluntary work.

*   Chao (2009) indicates a number of areas that may define an adult learner. These include age; cognitive maturity; employed, retired or unemployed status and career prospects; traditional or non-traditional learners. All of these labels can be attached to the term 'adult learners', as can the terms 'traditional' or 'non-traditional' learner.

• Darkenwald and Merriam (1982, p 9) define both the nature of adults and the purpose of adult learning in the following way:

Adult education is concerned not with preparing people for life, but rather helping people to live more successfully. Thus if there is to be an overarching function of the adult education enterprises, it is to assist adults to increase competence, or negotiate transitions, in their social roles (worker, parent, retiree), to help them gain greater fulfilment in their personal lives, and to assist them in solving personal and community problems.

You may wish to reflect on whether this view from 1982 is still representative today.

• Kidd (1978, p 17) suggests that:

[W]hat we describe as adult learning is not a different kind or order from child learning. Indeed our main point is that man must be seen as a whole, in his lifelong development. Principles of learning will apply, in ways that we shall suggest to all stages of life. The reason why we specify adults throughout is obvious. This is a field that has been neglected, not that of childhood.

We agree with this argument in the sense that learning is a lifelong process and that teachers need to not only be aware of the myriad 'issues' that these learners bring with them to the classroom but also be prepared to address these with a range of teaching strategies and resources. We explore these in greater detail in Chapters 4 to 6.

It is important for you, as it has been for us, to recognise your own learning journey.

Critical thinking activity

» To help you set the context in which you are teaching and supporting your adult learners, try to 'define' the following:

  – education;

  – training;

  – learning.

» Have you undertaken any education or training as an adult? What did you do? Where did you do it? And what, if anything, did you gain from it?

The following section, together with your reflections, should help you to understand and develop your own views of some of the terminology used.

What is education and where does it take place?

In developing your skills and knowledge for supporting adult learners it is important to consider carefully what you understand by the term 'education'. The term is often associated with the formal process of passing on knowledge, for example from an adult to children and young people. This is how we usually think about what takes place in schools, colleges or universities, where the effectiveness of the process is often tested by exams. This transfer of knowledge can be viewed by the pupils or students as something that is 'done to' them – a process in which they are passive recipients of learning. This is not a model we would want to apply to adult learning, in the context of which education could best be described as the sharing of knowledge, both theoretical and practical. It encompasses not only listening and learning and the sitting of formal exams, but also – and most importantly – collaborative learning and the sharing of knowledge, understanding, and skills for personal development.

Education for adult learners takes place in a wide range of settings, which can include:

*   **the local community** (community learning): learning takes place in the local community and is responsive to community needs. This could be in a village hall, local school or the FE college. The type of courses may include family learning and parenting skills, learning a sport or developing a hobby. There are a number of organisations that provide education in this context, such as the Workers' Educational Association (WEA) and the Women's Institute (WI);

*   **Further Education**: again, local colleges will provide a range of courses for adult learners. These may include courses that lead to formal qualifications for work-related purposes; courses that enable learners to develop skills and hobbies that may benefit both them and their community; access to Higher Education (HE) courses; and life skills provision for adults with learning difficulties;

*   **Higher Education**: this provides courses that lead to higher qualifications (Bachelor's degrees, Master's degrees) and professional qualifications, and continuous professional development;

*   **private training providers**: these often provide training that has been purchased by an employer and that is specifically tailored to meet their business requirements. It can take place in a number of locations including the business premises, local community venue or at the provider's own facilities.

What is training?

It is also important to understand the term 'training' as you may find you are working with adult learners in this context. This is often seen as learning a particular skill for a job. It has a practical and hence more vocational emphasis. This type of 'education' can often be viewed as a way of improving learners' employment prospects and helping them to extend their competence. Training normally takes place within the workplace or in a college of Further Education or indeed both.

What is learning?

This term embraces aspects of both education and training, but also much more. It is something that can happen within and away from the formal educational setting, and it happens throughout our lives. How often have we heard the phrase 'lifelong learning'? The National Adult Learning Survey (1998) defines the two main types of learning as follows:

*   formal taught learning: both in a classroom and in a practical situation, eg laying bricks, learning to swim, distance learning. These opportunities take place in a

variety of settings: at home, at an evening class, at a leisure centre or at a college or university;

- informal non-taught learning: studying on your own without joining a formal class. Learning by watching and talking to friends, colleagues and family.

Learning is at the heart of what we do as teachers. We, too, are always learning both formally and informally.

Working with adult learners

Whether you find yourself working with adults in a Further Education college, in an evening class or in a university, there are some things that most adult learners have in common:

- busy lives;
- the need for careful time management;
- access to resources;
- the ability to work collaboratively;
- wanting to be there; a desire to learn.

However, there are also areas of difference which are important to keep in mind. These include:

- types of qualification already held;
- level and source of motivation to learn;
- amount of time available for studying.

Who are we?

We are both experienced practitioners who have had our own unique learning journey to this point.

Jackie Scruton

I started my formal learning journey as an adult over 20 years ago. Like many adults I had attended a number of courses that were specifically connected to my work. But it was the support and interest from the head teacher of the school I worked in at that time which encouraged me to undertake further study, firstly in further and then Higher Education. The initial relationship with that head teacher and subsequently the building of a strong relationship with my MA tutor was very important to me as part of my learning journey. Without those relationships I would not have continued on my path. I recall that the tutors I worked with were very supportive and this was demonstrated by, for example, their responding to e-mails quickly and being available at 'odd' times for tutorials. I recognised that when studying as an adult the pressures of family life and work were hard to juggle, but it was interesting and challenging because of the encouragement and recognition of my working experiences by my tutors. This was illustrated on an occasion when one of my tutors, after carrying out a teaching observation, asked if they could come and teach that particular group of learners and did indeed do so. These were young adults with special educational needs. Clearly this was beyond what might be expected of a tutor's role. However, this had a lasting impression and has helped form the way in which I work with my adult learners. We discuss the importance of building relationships in Chapter 7.

I am also interested in using technology to support my learners and this stems from my own experiences as an adult learner. This technology and its use in education has grown enormously over the past 15 years. When I first started on my educational journey, things such as virtual learning environments and ebooks were not available. By the time I completed my Master's degree things had changed and I recognised and valued the use of such tools in order to support me in my studies. These experiences with the application of technology have given me the impetus to use them in my own teaching. If you are interested in developing your skills in the use of technology to support your learners then you will find Chapter 6 helpful.

Since the start of my teaching career I have taught adult learners in a variety of educational establishments. In Further Education I have taught subjects as diverse as basic skills and agricultural studies. I have also worked with adult learners who have identified special educational needs (SEN) including autistic spectrum disorder (ASD), specific learning difficulties (SPLD) and those with mental health difficulties. This has been both in a school setting and in a Further Education college. Recently I have been working in Higher Education teaching across a range of courses including traditional undergraduate courses with learners who are aged 18–21 and courses for adult learners returning to study. I also teach and supervise on Master's level courses and have run evening course for adults wanting to learn new skills in Makaton sign language. These experiences have helped me to understand the needs of adult learners and, in doing so, to develop the skills I feel are needed in order to support those learners.

Belinda Ferguson

My career in teaching adults began with teaching a professional qualification in the evenings in a Further Education college. I had no previous experience of teaching and, having obtained a science degree through the 'traditional route' of education, I needed a strategic and logical approach to teaching. On my teacher training course, the skills I learnt in developing lesson planning, assessing learners and giving feedback were particularly helpful to me as they gave me some direction in my teaching. If this is something that you want to develop too, you will find Chapter 4 useful. After I had gained experience in teaching, I made a bold decision to give up my full-time job and take up an assortment of sessional teaching opportunities at various different institutions ranging from short one-day courses to longer qualifications. It was a big risk, particularly as I had a young child to support, but I never regretted it as it gave me so much experience in teaching in a wide range of settings and with a variety of adult learners. As I developed my new career, I started to see the difference that education has on adults and the opportunities that it opens up. I became involved in teacher training for post-compulsory education and found that supporting teachers new to the sector was highly rewarding. I was able to share the experiences that I had gained from both my own teaching and through undertaking lesson observations of other teachers. We have interwoven our own experiences and those of our students and trainees into this book in the hope that you can benefit from them too.

I went on to study for my MA in education whilst working full-time and supporting a family and so I had to juggle many demands. Luckily I followed this course with a colleague and found the opportunities to discuss our new knowledge and ideas invaluable as it helped me to consolidate and understand in greater depth what I had learnt. We discuss the value of peer support in Chapter 7 and I hope that you will find this helpful too. My career has developed and I am now working at a university, still teaching adult learners as well as younger full-time undergraduates, and I am mentoring lecturers who are new to teaching in the HE sector. I work with a proactive team and we have many conversations about how we can support our students better in a way that helps them to succeed but also allows them to be autonomous learners. The conversation at the beginning of this introduction is typical of what you may hear when walking past the office. We hope that you can learn from our experiences. The focus that we have borne in mind throughout writing this book has been *what would have helped me when I first started teaching?* We hope this helps *you*.

How to use this book

By picking up this book you have demonstrated your interest in developing your skills and knowledge to support the adults with whom you are working or are planning to work. There is no right or wrong way of using it, but we have written it in an order that we hope will be helpful to you.

Chapters 1 to 3 explore how you can develop an understanding of your learners. This includes examining the background to adult learning and the types of adult learners you might teach. It also discusses motivation: what it is and how to encourage it in your learners. We also introduce you to stories of students and tutors. These illustrate some of the concepts we explored and that are referred to throughout the book.

Chapters 4 to 6 examine a range of strategies that you can you use to further support your learners in their studies. These include areas such as room layout, use of ICT, planning lessons and strategies to engage your learners, and activities to help build confidence.

Chapter 7 provides you with more detailed case studies and the opportunity to critically reflect on what you have learnt and how you might put this into practice.

There are two areas in particular that we would like to draw your attention to. The first is the critical thinking activities, which are designed to help you engage with the material and, more importantly, think about your own views and practices. Our busy working lives mean that often we do not have time for reflection, so by taking time to reflect whilst reading the book you will be better able to understand and engage with each topic and apply it to your own teaching. Secondly the student/tutor stories have been written to help illustrate some of the key points that we want to make. You may find it helpful to read these first, so that you get to know the 'characters' and start to relate to them. These can be found in Chapter 2.

And finally ...

We hope that you will find this a practical text that explores both theory and strategies relating to working with your adult learners, and that it will enable you to develop the skills and knowledge that will support these learners to succeed.

Taking it further

Other books in this series will help you to further develop your understanding of what it means to work with adult learners, in particular Sheine Peart's (2014) book *Equality and Diversity in Further Education*. In it she discusses how you might overcome barriers to inclusion and create a positive learning environment.

If you are interested in developing and understanding your reflective practice then *Teaching and Learning through Reflective Practice* by Tony Ghaye (2011) and *The Lifelong Learning Sector Reflective Reader* edited by Susan Wallace (2010) will support you.

Full references for these titles are provided below.

References

Chao, R (2009) *Understanding the Adult Learners' Motivation and Barriers to Learning.* Available at: www.academia.edu/1267765/Understanding_the_Adult_Learners_Motivation_and_Barriers_to_Learning

Darkenwald, G and Merriam, S B (1982) *Adult Education. Foundations of Practice.* New York: Harper and Row.

Ghaye, T (2011) *Teaching and Learning through Reflective Practice.* Abingdon: Routledge.

Gravells, A and Simpson, S (2012) *Equality and Diversity in the Lifelong Learning Sector.* 2nd Edition. London: Learning Matters.

Gray, D et al. (2000) *Training to Teach in Adult and Further Education.* Cheltenham: Nelson Thornes.

Kidd, J (1978) *How Adults Learn.* Englewood Cliffs, NJ: Prentice Hall Regents.

Knowles, M et al. (1984) *Andragogy in Action. Applying Modern Principles of Adult Education.* San Francisco: Jossey Bass.

Peart, S (2014) *Equality and Diversify in Further Education.* Northwich: Critical Publishing.

Rogers, A and Horrocks, N (2010) *Teaching Adults.* 4th Edition. Maidenhead: Open University Press.

Wallace, S (2010) (ed) *The Lifelong Learning Sector Reflective Reader.* Exeter: Learning Matters.

Wlodkowski, R (1999) *Enhancing Adult Motivation to Learn.* San Fransisco: Jossey-Bass.

1 The context of adult learning

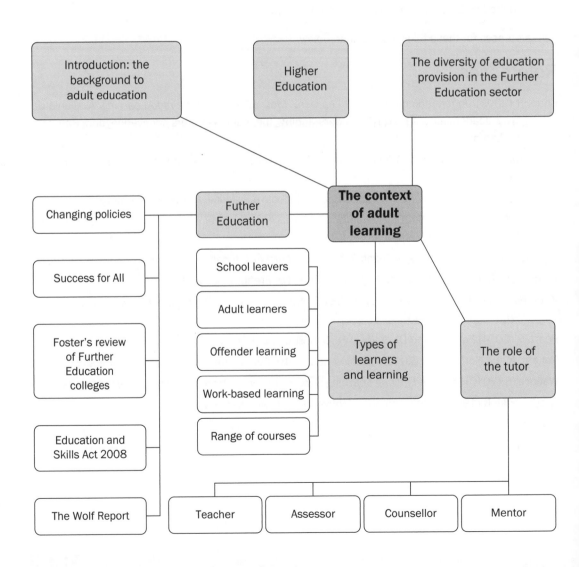

Chapter aims

This chapter briefly explores the diversity of the post-compulsory education and training sector. It considers the types of learners that you may find; the range of courses that they might be studying and the variety of levels; where they may be learning; and the roles that you as a tutor may need to fulfil.

By the end of the chapter you will be able to:

* identify the background and development of post-compulsory education;

* reflect on the implications of policy changes for managers in post-compulsory education;

* recognise the diversity of learners in post-compulsory education;

* identify the range of courses and levels that are studied in post-compulsory education;

* explain the varied roles of the tutor.

Introduction: the background to adult education

The scope of post-compulsory education is vast and you may hear numerous terms associated with it. An overarching term often used is 'lifelong learning' – this refers to learning that can take place after formal education and includes: post-compulsory education or training, vocational skills or education, adult education, continuing education and continuing professional development. In education terms, due to funding streams that are linked to ages of learners, adults are often defined as being over 19 years of age. Mature learners are usually considered to be over 21. Educational establishments may receive additional funding for mature learners and can be more flexible in their admissions criteria. The reasons that the scope of this sector is so vast can be understood by examining some of the changes that have occurred.

In 1992 the Further and Higher Education Act resulted in Further Education colleges becoming freestanding incorporated bodies, no longer under the control of local education authorities. The Act set out the purpose of the Further Education sector, which was to provide full-time education for 16–18-year-olds; part-time and full-time education for those over 18; and to provide education for people with learning difficulties. Anyone who looks into the doors of a Further Education college these days will see that the scope of learners is much greater than this now. A tutor in Further Education can expect to have learners who are aged 14, currently in full-time compulsory education at a local secondary school but who are attending college for one or two days a week to develop vocational skills; 16–18-year-olds taking GCSEs, A levels, vocational certificates, diplomas and extended diplomas; as well as adults between 18 and over 80 on a variety of courses ranging from professional to personal interest.

In 1996 Tomlinson released a report that aimed to improve educational opportunities for about 130,000 people who attended Further Education colleges and other centres. He made a number of proposals to be implemented over the following two years and further proposals for changes over a 5–10-year timescale. His particular focus was on inclusive learning. The report identified that students with learning difficulties or disabilities received a lower quality of learning opportunities compared to their peers and that some groups of learners were not properly represented in Further Education. As a result of these findings, the committee recommended a *redesigning of the very process of learning, assessment and organisation so as to fit the objectives and learning styles of the student* (FEFC, 2006, p 4). This was one of the many reviews and reports that have been prepared about the Further and Higher Education sectors to establish their role and place in education.

Further Education

The role of the Further Education sector has been explored and debated over the last 20 years. This section looks at some of the key policies and developments that have occurred and the impact they have had.

Critical thinking activity

As you read this section, reflect on the recommendations of the different reports.

» *Do you notice any recurring themes?*

» *If you were a college manager, how would you respond and decide what your priorities are?*

Changing policies

The purpose of the Further Education sector and its funding mechanism has been regularly reviewed since 1992. A Green Paper launched The Learning Age consultation in 1998, setting out the following principles:

- investing in learning to benefit everyone;
- lifting barriers to learning;
- putting people first;
- sharing responsibilities with employers, employees and the community;
- achieving world-class standards and value for money; and
- working together as the key to success.

(DfEE, 1998a)

At the same time, *The Learning Age: Further Education for the New Millennium* (DfEE, 1998b) was published, which set out the government's response to a review into widening participation, chaired by Baroness Helena Kennedy. It aimed to encourage and engage those who had not traditionally taken advantage of educational opportunities, in particular those with no or limited qualifications. The intention was to enable people to break out of a cycle of economic and social exclusion. The government committed to additional funding to provide opportunities for a further 80,000 students in Further Education, with the focus on the *educationally disadvantaged population*. Learning opportunities were extended to people who would not otherwise have had the chance to learn by providing for an extra 500,000 people in further and Higher Education by 2002. Education and training was to be more flexible and accessible for all, and barriers to learning were to be removed through the introduction of Individual Learning Accounts (ILAs) to help those with low skills or low pay. The quality, responsiveness and local accountability of FE colleges were to be improved and a better-focused careers service would enhance information on learning and related career opportunities. The paper also sought to rebalance the partnership for investment in learning between the government, individuals and employers (DfEE, 1998b).

The Individual Learning Accounts were launched in 2000 but abandoned in October 2001 following concerns about fraud and abuse. Education Maintenance Allowance (EMA), introduced in 2004, was a financial scheme for students between the ages of 16 and 19 whose parents' household income was below a certain level. It was intended to contribute towards the cost of travel and books needed for study with the purpose of increasing participation in FE. This scheme was cancelled in 2010 following budget cuts and criticisms, and was replaced by a bursary scheme.

Success for All

In the Success for All (DfES, 2002) strategy, Further Education and training were identified as having a vital role in *achieving the goal of a learning society*. The providers identified in this were Further Education and sixth form colleges, schools with sixth forms, local authority adult education institutions, and private and voluntary sectors. It was stated that this diverse learning and skills sector would provide a wide range of opportunities for millions of learners, thousands of businesses and every community in the country. This strategy recognised issues that arose out of the incorporation of colleges in 1993 and suggested that there was a lack of focus and strategic planning in colleges, as well as varying quality of provision, a legacy of underinvestment in infrastructure and the neglect of career development of staff. However, it was recognised that Further Education colleges had an important role to play in their communities with a commitment to social inclusion and widening participation for their learners. The government set out the goals of the Success for All strategy as being: meeting needs and improving choice; putting teaching and learning at the heart of what we do; developing the teachers and leaders of the future; and developing a framework for quality and success. One aspect of this was to drive excellence for 14–19-year-olds and to set out the collaboration between schools and colleges to provide vocational opportunities at Key Stage 4 of compulsory education. It also identified the need to extend provision of Higher Education and widen choices for 14–19-year-olds.

Foster's review of Further Education colleges

In 2005 Sir Andrew Foster undertook a review of the future of Further Education colleges, *Realising the Potential: A review of the future role of further education colleges*. His conclusions were wide reaching, but in general he stated that the FE sector lacked a clear purpose and that colleges were not generally realising their potential. He identified that there was confusion about the funding available and the aspirations of colleges, with too many students failing to pass the course they had enrolled on. Foster claimed that the FE sector was not seen as purposeful but as a *middle child* between schools and Higher Education (Foster et al., 2005, viii). One of Foster's proposals was to address the problem of FE's *casualised and ageing workforce* to increase the quality of provision in order to meet the demands of local employers. Foster's view was that the key purpose of FE was skills training. This was further confirmed in the White Paper *Further Education: Raising Skills, Improving Life Chances* (DIUS, 2007) which was the government's response to Foster's report. The impact on the sector was that its role was now defined as *developing skills for employment*. Many colleges revisited their vision, structure and curriculum content with this focus.

Education and Skills Act 2008

In 2008 the Education and Skills Act set out to improve the participation in learning for young people and adults by giving adults a second chance to gain skills needed to succeed in employment and by raising the participation in education or training leaving age to 18. The rationale for this was that it would provide more opportunities for young people through education and training and provide support to enable them to engage in learning. This further emphasises the role of the FE sector as a provider of skills training with a particular focus up to the age of 19.

The Wolf Report

The Wolf Report, published in 2011, was a review of pre-19 vocational education. The Report found that:

> many of England's 14–19 year olds do not, at present, progress successfully into either secure employment or higher-level education and training. Many of them leave education without the skills that will enable them to progress at a later date.
>
> (Wolf, 2011, p 8)

The Report made key recommendations. These were to:

- ensure that programmes of study equip young learners for the labour market or for educational progression, whether vocational or academic routes were taken;

- enable young people to make decisions by providing accurate and useful information about 14–19 education opportunities;

- simplify the 14–19 system and qualifications available to enable young people to receive accurate information;

- free up resources for teaching and learning, and allow innovation and efficiency to be encouraged.

With effect from September 2013, the law stipulated that all students are required to continue in education or training until their eighteenth birthday. Education or training is defined as full-time study in a school, college or with a training provider; full-time work or volunteering combined with part-time education or training; or an apprenticeship (DfE, 2013).

These reviews highlight the change in focus from adults to a greater emphasis on 14–19-year-olds to improve the employment opportunities at age 19. The impact on adult learners has been that funding previously available to subsidise the cost of studying has been directed to 14–19-year-olds. This has resulted in less financial support for adults and a higher cost of the courses that they may study. This can result in lower participation or can cause a barrier to learning and progression for adults.

Higher Education

In contrast to the numerous changes to the FE sector, HE has not been subject to so many frequent policies and reviews, but it has had to respond to the changes in FE, particularly in relation to curriculum and qualification reviews. However, HE has seen some significant changes itself. The 1992 Further and Higher Education Act resulted in former polytechnics being granted university status, removing the polytechnic/university divide. However, a distinction still exists as universities are often classed as 'pre 1992 and post 1992' or 'old' and 'new' universities. The Act also introduced tuition fees for students. As previously discussed, *The Learning Age: Further Education for the New Millennium* (DfEE, 1998b) had a particular focus on widening participation which aimed to increase and facilitate the involvement in Higher Education of under-represented groups. Many interventions and strategies were introduced to achieve target figures that were set. Foundation degrees were seen as an ideal qualification which links academic study with employability. These are intermediate degrees, a work-related Higher Education qualification combining academic and work-related learning. They are offered at many Further Education colleges which provide access to Higher Education in a local environment. Foundation degrees are usually validated by a Higher Education institution (HEI). This encouraged staff in Further Education colleges to form alliances with local HEIs and required a new skill set for teachers to learn to teach and assess a higher level of qualification than they may have been used to.

The 2004 Higher Education Act enabled HEIs to set their own tuition fees up to a specified basic amount. The Office for Fair Access (OFFA) was created with a remit to approve and monitor plans where institutions wished to charge fees above the basic amount. These plans stipulated how HEIs would develop financial support packages and bursaries for students from lower income backgrounds and other under-represented groups to ensure that widening participation was still maintained.

The Department for Business Innovation and Skills produced a policy in 2012 in which a new system of funding for Higher Education was established which had the purpose of creating a more diverse and competitive Higher Education sector requiring graduates to make a much larger contribution to their education. This saw the annual tuition fees for students increase dramatically, possibly causing some to question the need for Higher Education. However, after an initial reduction in university applications following the introduction of this policy, overall undergraduate applications do not appear to have been affected.

Critical thinking activity

Initiatives have been in place to encourage more individuals from low income backgrounds and other under-represented groups to participate in Higher Education.

» *What are the barriers to participating in Higher Education?*

» *What strategies do you think could overcome these?*

The diversity of education provision in the Further Education sector

By looking at the reforms and initiatives in Further Education, you will realise that the types of learners and the range of courses and qualifications are diverse. The environment where learning takes place is not restricted to a college or university institution but is much more varied. This diversity requires the tutor to be flexible and responsive to the learner's needs and to ensure that they are provided with a positive learning experience.

Types of learners and learning

We will now examine the range of learners that you may encounter in Further Education. When reading the following section, try to envisage the challenges that these learners need to overcome when participating in education, and what your role is in supporting them to do that.

School leavers

A large number of students in an FE college will be 16-year-old school leavers who have moved from a structured school learning environment with a regular timetable. On entering Further Education they may be faced with many new challenges and they will need to be supported in these. They may be encountering an environment that is much larger and busier than their previous place of learning, one in which they can easily get lost. There will be areas that feel quite intimidating, such as a library or a canteen. The timetable is very likely to be different from a regular school timetable with longer lessons and longer days and no school bell to indicate when they need to be in class. They will have more free study time and they may not know how to utilise this. The type of learning will be different from a school environment and school leavers will need their learning 'scaffolding'. This involves creating a support structure for them while they develop skills for independent learning.

Adult learners

Adult learners will be any learners from age 19 upwards. They may be studying part time or full time for a variety of reasons. Adult learners may be returning to learning after a short or long break in their education. Their aim may be to improve their career prospects, to be able to support their children, to update their skills or to study for general interest. Adult learners face many challenges – the main ones being confidence and time management. We will explore these in more detail throughout this book.

A college can be an intimidating place for an adult and this may prevent many people from participating. Programmes have been established to take learning into the community rather than expecting learners to go to a college. Some schools provide facilities for family learning; community centres and other organisations also provide useful locations where courses can be delivered in the local community. Such arrangements are well placed to increase the participation of adults in education but they do limit the resources that are available to the learner and teacher. The style of learning is more informal than in a college environment and learners may be more easily distracted, so strategies to fully engage them are required.

Adult learners have different needs and priorities which we will be discussing throughout this book.

Offender learning

There are many learning opportunities available in prison environments when people are serving a sentence or, possibly, for people on remand. Historically the courses on offer have been focused on improving adult literacy and numeracy, social skills and ICT. However, the scope is wider than this and can extend to personal interest, vocational and courses for employment. A tutor working in a prison will find that the environment is very different to that traditionally used for teaching and learning. Classrooms are usually within a designated building, and teaching will rarely be undertaken in the prison wings. This enables the students to attend in a structured and formalised way. The resources that are available will be limited, although a security protected virtual learning environment may be provided.

The aim of offender learning programmes is to give offenders in prison access to learning and skills to enable them to gain qualifications and skills for employment and have a positive role in society (OLASS, http://olass.skillsfundingagency.bis.gov.uk/). A number of Further Education colleges deliver accredited programmes to offenders in prisons or the community.

Work-based learning

Work-based learning can cover many facets of learning for work. It includes programmes that support unemployed people into work, apprenticeships, skills and knowledge training, and academic qualifications undertaken within or relating to the workplace. Historically there have been a number of programmes to support people back to or into work, such as New Deals and Employment Zones. In June 2011 the Work Programme was launched. Its aim was to help people who are at risk of becoming long-term unemployed to find work. The programme is delivered in the private, public and voluntary sectors. Service providers are paid almost entirely on results, which are defined as job outcomes. The longer a participant stays in work, the more the provider gets paid. The longer a participant has been unemployed, and the fewer skills they have, the greater the payment that provider will receive once they have secured employment (Department for Work and Pensions, 2011). The incentive for providers is to find suitable and appropriate ways to support the participant in achieving sustainable employment, and the Work Programme is designed to allow providers to exercise flexibility and innovation in their approach without government restrictions.

Apprenticeships, which are available to anybody over the age 16, give people the opportunity to work for an employer for 30 hours per week, earn a salary and obtain a qualification. The National Apprenticeship Service supports, funds and co-ordinates apprenticeships in England, with over 150,000 employers offering apprenticeships at three different levels: intermediate, advanced and higher level. Apprenticeships will last a minimum of 12 months and lead to a recognised qualification. The subject areas in which apprenticeships can be undertaken are vast and include agriculture, education, construction, health and public services. Apprentices may study in an FE college alongside their employment, or they may study with a private trainer or employer.

Adults in employment often undertake further learning to advance their career prospects or to gain qualifications in their current field. This is referred to as continuing professional development. This may be wholly or partially funded by an employer or self-funded by the learner themselves. Adults are usually self-motivated to be successful, but they may exhibit anxieties and concerns about their learning and experience, many of which are discussed in later chapters of this book. Work-based learning courses can vary in length and level – they may range from short courses to long postgraduate qualifications. The nature of these courses means learners develop knowledge relating to their own work and can apply it to their work practice. This is the essence of vocational qualifications and foundation degrees. Some professions have mandatory continuing professional development.

Work-based learning also includes mandatory training that employers arrange for their employees to attend and is a requirement for the job. Examples of such training courses are: manual handling, handling and lifting, food hygiene, first aid, and an array of health and safety courses. These courses may last from a few hours to several days and may be delivered on the employer's premises or off-site. They can become a 'tick box' exercise where the training may not be taken seriously by the employee or employer. The skill in delivering these courses is to motivate and engage the learners by keeping the content relevant and relatable to their work practice.

The Workers' Educational Association (WEA), founded in 1903, is a charity that provides 9,500 courses in England and Scotland. The particular focus is on providing educational opportunities for adults who face social and economic disadvantages with the aim of providing them with confidence to learn new skills, engage in society by becoming active citizens, live healthy lives and broaden their horizons. The curriculum includes employability, health and well-being, art, history, languages, ICT, community engagement and culture. The mission of the WEA is to:

> develop educational opportunities for the most disadvantaged in society; raise educational aspirations; ensure opportunities exist for adults to return to learning; bring great teaching and education to local communities, and involve students and WEA supporters as active members to build an educational movement for social purpose.
>
> (WEA, 2013, p 4)

A report in 2013 exploring the impact of WEA suggests that it is successful in achieving this mission.

Critical thinking activity

Consider the terms 'teaching', 'tutoring' and 'training'.

»   *Do you think these terms mean different things?*

»   *If so, describe what you think they mean and what impact this might have on performing these roles.*

Range of courses

A wide range of learners engage in post-compulsory education for a number of reasons. If you look through a prospectus or at any FE college website, you will see the scope of courses that are offered at a variety of levels of difficulty. An FE tutor may need to adapt their teaching style to different levels, so it is important to know what these levels are.

Critical thinking activity

»   *Fill in the final column in Table 1.1 below to identify the target age group of learners for the qualification shown.*

Table 1.1 Levels of courses

National qualification framework level	Equivalent to	Target age group of learner
Entry	Entry level awards, certificates and diplomas; Foundation Learning Tier pathways; Functional Skills at entry level; Entry level certificates; Skills for Life at entry level	
Level 1	GCSE grades G to D; BTEC awards level 1; Functional Skills level 1; OCR Nationals; Foundation Learning Tier pathways; Key Skills level 1; Skills for Life; NVQs level 1	
Level 2	GCSE grades C to A*; BTEC awards, certificates and diplomas at level 2; Functional Skills level 2; Key Skills level 2; Higher Diploma; Skills for Life; NVQs level 2	
Level 3	AS/A levels; International Baccalaureate Diploma; Key Skills level 3; NVQs level 3; BTEC diplomas level 3; BTEC Nationals, OCR Nationals; Advanced and Progression Diploma; Access to HE Diploma	

National qualification framework level	Equivalent to	Target age group of learner
Level 4	Year 1 Bachelor degree; Higher National Certificate (HNC); First year foundation degree; Certificates of Higher Education; BTEC professional diplomas; Key Skills level 4; NVQs level 4	
Level 5	Year 2 Bachelor degree; Higher National Diplomas (HND); Final year foundation degree Diplomas of Higher Education; NVQs level 4*	
Level 6	Bachelor degrees; graduate certificates and diplomas; professional diplomas, certificates and awards; NVQs level 4*	
Level 7	Postgraduate certificates and diplomas; Master's degree; Advanced professional awards; Fellowship and fellowship diplomas NVQs level 5*	
Level 8	Doctorates NVQs level 5*	

Source: Ofqual 2012

The reality is that all of the above qualifications are suited for all adult learners depending on their aspirations and needs.

All courses with a formal qualification will be delivered and assessed at a certain level according to this framework. Whilst most of the learners in a group will be learning at the same level, it is not uncommon to have learners in a group working at two different levels. It will take skill on the part of the tutor to manage this learning process and ensure that all learners are taught, challenged and assessed appropriately according to the level at which they are studying. It is important that you familiarise yourself with the levels at which the courses you teach are being delivered and ensure that you know what this means in terms of the quality of work that you should expect from your learners. You will need to then ensure that you deliver your lessons at the appropriate level required so that it is aligned with the course outcomes. This is explored further in Chapter 4.

The role of the tutor

From exploring the wide diversity of learners and the range of courses, you can see that the role of the tutor is complex and demanding. Not only do tutors need to have a thorough and current understanding of their subject, they need to develop suitable skills in teaching and supporting their learners. The first stage in this is to understand the needs and challenges of the learners they encounter. This is explored further in Chapter 6.

Teacher

Tutors need to learn how to plan their teaching to ensure that it is delivered in a suitable and structured way. This will entail identifying course and module learning outcomes and designing lessons that support the learner in meeting these. This is examined in Chapter 4. The level of learning will impact on the role of the tutor. Whilst learners studying courses at lower levels may need a higher level of instruction or support, learners at higher levels will need a tutor who facilitates and supports a learning environment that enables the learners themselves to take more responsibility for their learning.

Assessor

Assessing learning is part of the learning process and it is a key requirement in students demonstrating their skills and knowledge. Some courses require continual formal assessment and may entail the tutor undertaking an assessor's qualification. Most commonly, but not exclusively, such courses are NVQs (National Vocational Qualifications) which are qualifications designed to ascertain learners' performance in work-related tasks. The purpose of assessment is to identify the learners' performance and to provide constructive feedback to help them improve. This needs to be done in a way that the learner can understand and incorporate into their work. As these qualifications are assessed on an individual basis, they will need to be verified by a qualified internal verifier (from the same organisation) and an external verifier (from the awarding body).

Counsellor

The tutor will often need to support their learners through difficult or challenging times and they will need to have patience and counselling skills to be able to guide the learner to further support. It is important to recognise and keep to boundaries and seek additional guidance to ensure that the learner is supported appropriately. We discuss this more in Chapter 6.

Mentor

Depending on the type of course and the age of the learner, tutors may find themselves in a mentoring role. Gravells and Wallace (2007, p 15) explain that mentoring involves providing support for someone through a period of transition from one stage of development to another. They go on to identify that it is a *process of change and development that goes deeper than simply acquiring more knowledge*. We can see then that this role is not just about teaching or learning, but supporting people in their personal and professional development. You may find yourself in a position of mentoring your colleagues who are new to teaching or in a new role and will require a structure of support to allow the mentee to identify and learn about their responsibilities and develop skills through the identification of personal action planning. Indeed, in your early teaching career, you will probably be assigned a mentor to support you in your development. In addition to the mentoring of colleagues, FE tutors may also find themselves in a mentoring role with their students.

Critical thinking activity

» *Thinking about the various roles of the tutor, identify how many different roles you are required to fulfil.*

» *How do you prioritise and manage these? Explain your answers.*

Chapter reflections

In this chapter we have seen how government policies and initiatives have influenced and changed the focus of the FE and HE sectors. This in turn has an impact on the curriculum and qualifications offered and the skills needed to teach and support learners in those sectors. The focus of FE has moved from adult education to the development of skills in 14–19-year-olds, which has had an impact of the diversity and availability of courses and funding for adults. However, widening participation and increased costs of Higher Education have resulted in the growth of Higher Education courses in FE colleges, which in turn brings in a new type of adult learner. We have explored the range of levels of courses and types of qualifications which require tutors to familiarise themselves with different teaching and assessment needs. This places demands on tutors as they will have to develop the appropriate skills and flexibility to support their adult learners to reach their maximum potential.

Taking it further

If you would like to find out more about the changes and diversity in post-compulsory education and the impact of government policy, you may find Anne O'Grady's (2013) book *Lifelong Learning In the UK* interesting.

You may also like to access the following documents:

Department for Business, Innovation and Skills (2012) *Making the Higher Education System More Efficient and Diverse*. Available at: www.gov.uk/government/policies/making-the-higher-education-system-more-efficient-and-diverse

Higher Education Act 2004. Available at: www.legislation.gov.uk/ukpga/2004/8/notes/contents

National Apprenticeships Service (2009–2014). Available at: www.apprenticeships.org.uk

References

Department for Education (DfE) (2013) *Raising the Participation Age* (RPA). Available at: www.education.gov.uk/childrenandyoungpeople/youngpeople/participation/rpa

DfEE (1998a) *The Learning Age: A Renaissance for New Britain*. Available at: www.lifelonglearning.co.uk/greenpaper/index.htm

DfEE (1998b) *The Learning Age: Further Education for the New Millennium*. Available at: www.lifelonglearning.co.uk/kennedy/index.htm

DfES (2002) *Success for All: Reforming Further Education and Training*. Available at: http://dera.ioe.ac.uk/4568/1/success-for-all-reforming-further-education-and-training.pdf

DIUS (2007) *Further Education: Raising Skills, Improving Life Chances*. London: Department for Innovations, Universities and Skills.

Department for Work and Pensions (DWP) (2011) The Work Programme. Available at: www.gov.uk/government/uploads/system/uploads/attachment_data/file/49884/the-work-programme.pdf

Further Education Funding Council (FEFC) (2006) *Inclusive Learning: Report of the Learning Difficulties and/or Disability Committee*. Coventry.

Foster, A et al. (2005) *Realising the Potential: A Review of the Future Role of Further Education Colleges*. Annesley: DFES Publications.

Gravells, J and Wallace, S (2007) *Mentoring*. 2nd Edition. Exeter: Learning Matters.

Offender Learning Skills Service (OLASS). Available at: http://olass.skillsfundingagency.bis.gov.uk/

Office of Qualifications and Examinations Regulations (Ofqual). Available at: http://ofqual.gov.uk/qualifications-and-assessments/qualification-frameworks/

O'Grady, A (2013) *Lifelong Learning in the UK: An Introductory Guide for Education studies*. Abingdon: Routledge.

Wolf, A (2011) *Review of Vocational Education: The Wolf Report*. Available at: www.gov.uk/government/publications/review-of-vocational-education-the-wolf-report

Workers' Educational Association (2013) *Impact of WEA Education*. Executive Summary Report May 2013. Available at: www.wea.org.uk/

2 Learner and tutor stories

Chapter aims

This chapter provides you with learner and tutor 'stories'. Throughout the book we have referred to these stories and they have been written to help you to develop your understanding of some of the complexities of teaching and supporting adult learners. These stories are based on events we have been involved in or have observed, and as such provide you with real situations to reflect on.

By the end of the chapter you will be able to:

- identify a number of difficulties that adult learners may experience both inside and outside your classroom;

- identify issues that you as a tutor may face when working with adult learners;

- understand more clearly how to support your adult learners.

Learner stories

Critical thinking activity

»   As you read through the stories below, identify and reflect on the key issues for both the learners and their teachers. Make a list or table of these so that you can compare it to our own at the end of the chapter.

CASE STUDY

Ed: male, in his 30s

My name is Ed and I am doing a foundation degree at a Further Education college. I have a full-time job and a young family at home, so studying part-time in the evening is the only way that I can gain further qualifications. I need to do the course because I want to move out of the job I am in and I hope that it will give me a chance to apply for better jobs. When I enrolled to do the course, I was really nervous about returning to studying and unsure that I would be good enough. The things that worried me most were: finding time to read, being able to understand the work, and whether I would be able to finish the course. At the first lesson, I thought all the other learners seemed really confident and I felt out of place. It was really difficult to make friends and I wondered for quite a while whether I had done the right thing by starting the course. I doubted whether I could do assignments and didn't know how to start or what was expected and I was nervous about asking for help. After about six or seven weeks, the tutors made us give feedback to another student about an assignment idea. I was really unsure about doing this as I thought my views were not worth anything and I didn't want someone else to see my ideas because I thought I wasn't clever enough. However, it turned out really well as the other student thought my ideas were good, and I realised that I was able to help somebody else and make useful comments. It was at this point that I realised that I could do this and I started feel a bit more positive. It also helped me to talk to other learners, which helped me to realise that we were all feeling the same.

The fears and anxieties that Ed had are common amongst many adult learners. Now James discusses some of his experiences of returning to learn alongside younger students.

CASE STUDY

James: male, in his 40s

I was recently made redundant from my job, and after I had difficulty getting another job in the field I decided to reskill and enrolled on a course at my local college. I was really nervous about returning to learning again and the thought of learning alongside other students *much younger than me was daunting. I have to say though that the tutor made the whole experience much easier than I thought it would be. When I went into the classroom on the first day, he was smiling and seemed friendly. The tables were laid out in a horseshoe shape so we could all see each other, which was not what I was expecting. I thought it would be more formal, particularly based on my experiences at school and work. There were also name cards for us to put our forenames on so we could start to learn each other's names. The tutor collected these up at the end of each lesson and gave them out at the start of the next – this lasted for several weeks. I noticed that the tutor always addressed us by name and encouraged us to use each other's names too. Thinking back, this really helped us to build friendships from the start which was great and I felt that the age difference did not matter. The younger students seemed to respect me and I found that I respected them too. It also helped us to build a good relationship with the tutor, which became particularly important for me later on.*

Part-way through the second term of the course, my wife became very ill and I needed to support her and look after our two young children. Although I attended college as often as I could, I didn't have much time to study at home and felt under pressure to earn an income, but I really wanted to complete the course. My tutor was very supportive. I was able to work with him to set realistic targets for my assignments. He was understanding and encouraging and didn't allow me to just give up. Without his support I would not have finished the course. My peers were also surprisingly supportive and helpful, especially given their age. One even offered to babysit for me so I could study! I am sure that it must have been the way that the tutor got us to get to know each other in the beginning, and the way we worked together as a group that created that environment.

It hasn't been an easy time, I have been under a lot of stress and pressure, but just knowing that my tutor was understanding and would help me to see a way through has been so important. He also contacted student services who were able to investigate any additional funding that I could get, which was really helpful as I didn't know where to start. It has been worth it all now that I have my new qualification and a new job!

James' initial induction into the course was a positive experience which enabled a good community of learning to be established. Compare this with Mateusz's experience. He did not find the induction and beginning of the course helpful.

CASE STUDY

Mateusz: male, aged 19

I wasn't keen about starting my course. I only enrolled on it as I couldn't get a decent job and my parents pushed me into it. It seemed the best option out of them all, but I wasn't interested in the subject, I don't like studying or exams. I had a part-time job working 20 hours a week in the college canteen – washing up, cleaning tables and so on. Nothing exciting but the money was okay. This college is where the course was being taught so at least I could continue working whilst doing the course. Although my friends say I am very opinionated and confident, I didn't feel like that at school. I never felt that I was allowed to have my own views and this made me doubt my abilities.

The course started okay, but as it was busy in the canteen my employer would often ask me to do extra shifts when I was in college. The money was useful and as the lessons were boring I chose to work, but then I started missing a lot of lessons. It was difficult to know what to do. After about the fourth week the pace of the course picked up, having been slow at the start. It became more interesting as the lessons seemed to have a purpose. The tutors explained what we would be doing in the lesson and why we were doing it. It all seemed to make sense to me. At the end of the lesson we would go back over what we had learned in class and this made me feel like I had actually achieved something and I wanted to do more, so I started turning down the extra canteen work. It wasn't always like this – there were still some boring lessons which were a waste of time, but more of them were fun. One week we were given a topic to research and prepare for a debate in the next lesson. This was brilliant! The debate was done properly, with rules and that, but we were allowed to give our own opinions, even though we did have to explain them clearly. It was good fun and I realised that the subject could actually be quite interesting and I could be good at it. I didn't even mind reading about the subject for the debate. I hope we continue to do more of this next year.

Inclusive teaching and learning strategies have obviously engaged and motivated Mateusz in his studies. Although she had different concerns, Hadas found that inclusive strategies, such as the use of technology, were essential in enabling her progress.

CASE STUDY

Hadas: female, in her early 50s

My name is Hadas and I am studying at my local FE college. I have spent 25 years looking after my children and now they are all grown up and have left home. They have children of their own and none of them live locally any more. Over the last year I have had a lot of time to think about what I would like to do for 'me'. Six months ago I saw a poster on a bus advertising access courses. I am now on one of these courses at my local Further Education college. I am not sure what I want to do after the course, but I am enjoying doing something just for me, so much so that I have also joined the evening course 'learning to cook' at my local secondary school.

The first thing that worried me was how I was going to find the money for the fees. I had to borrow money from my family, so now I feel under pressure to do well. It is a long time since I have studied and I was very nervous on the first evening. I need not have worried – the tutor was very nice. He took time to tell us all about himself and the course. He then asked us to share things about ourselves. This was done in small groups and helped me to get know some of the other people on the course. In the following weeks I have sat with them and we have shared our worries and also things we have found that help us with our studying.

I was also anxious about using technology, especially the computer. I could send e-mails and look up things on Google, but sometimes I heard phrases like 'click on'. I was not sure what they meant and was worried about asking and feeling stupid. However, in the first few weeks the tutor always used the whiteboard to show us how to access things. It was just part of his lesson, but because he did it every week it became familiar. Then every week he set us tasks that we had to do in our own time. To finish the tasks I had to use the internet and the college's own website. When I had done the task I had to upload it the website. This gave me plenty of practice and I have become much more confident in using the technology. It also helped me to see how well I was doing as he gave me feedback each week on the task. My progress has been an issue for me especially as I have borrowed money. My family keep asking me 'When will you be qualified?' I can tell them what the tutor has told me and this has helped me to feel more confident.

This example shows how some problems can be solved easily, which helped to build Hadas' confidence. Ben had different challenges, but again you can see how the tutor was instrumental in motivating him by drawing on his existing skills and knowledge.

CASE STUDY

Ben: male, in his mid-20s

My name is Ben and I am a part-time student at my local FE college. I am studying an NVQ level 3 in care, having already completed both my level 1 and 2. I have a full-time job which involves working a shift pattern. I love using social networking sites because they allow me to stay in touch with my friends and as a result I am happy to use technology in my studying. On my previous course I got very used to using things like e-portfolios, so now I find it easy. I have even bought a tablet to help on my new course. I really like one of my tutors as they set me very tough but realistic goals. This might be to read a book chapter on a topic I know little about but that is relevant to my studies, or to interview someone I work with. Once I had done the task they gave me feedback and then set me another one. More often than not this was linked to the previous task but it seemed a little harder. This really gave me the motivation to carry on and also gave me a thirst to continue exploring areas that I may not have been comfortable looking at in the past.

Looking back I had a great team of tutors working with me. Another tutor really understood that I had a range of work experiences that I could use to support my academic studies. In sessions she would go through some theory with us and then ask us to think about this in relation to our work. She encouraged us to talk to each other about our work and try to make links between what we were doing on a practical level and what she was talking to us about. It was great and enabled me to go back to work and think about what I did, why I did it and how to change things to make them better.

Tutor stories

CASE STUDY

Debbie: female, in her late 20s

I decided to start teaching in order to share my knowledge and experience of my subject with a new generation. I had no experience in teaching before I started and was just given classes to teach. I was completely thrown in at the deep end with little support. Colleagues told me that it was the best way to learn, but I felt so scared – I was sure that I would let the students down. I couldn't see what they could learn from me. Six months on and I am still scared, but I have noticed that the students keep coming to my lessons so they must like them and do seem to be learning a bit. Well, most of them. There are two students who are always chatting in class and are often late. It is very clear that they do not like me, so I avoid them. I just leave them to either do the work that I set or to chat. They don't seem to be bothering anyone else so it is their decision if they don't want to join in.

One day I plucked up the courage to talk to some of my colleagues. It was such a relief to talk to them. They told me that they had the same concerns as me when they started teaching, and when I told them that I felt such a fraud calling myself a teacher, they told me that they knew what I meant as they had felt exactly the same. One of them even said that she still feels like that after five years and is sure that she will get found out one day! This really helped me to see that my feelings were normal. They gave me advice about the students who don't like me. It turns out that one of them has family problems and is probably offloading to her friend in class. They helped me to realise that by ignoring them, I am giving them the time and opportunity to do this. They suggested that I interacted more with them and give them targets in the lesson to help them concentrate more. This is a good idea, but I am a bit nervous about approaching them after ignoring them all this time. I suppose I need to take responsibility for them and approach them. I'll do it next lesson.

The anxieties that Debbie feels are common, especially for new teachers. However, she needs to improve her understanding of the way adults behave. Andy is also a new teacher who, although confident in his subject matter, found classroom management problematic.

CASE STUDY

Andy: male, in his mid-40s

I decided to start teaching after a career change. I had been very confident in my previous career in recruitment but I found starting a lesson so hard. It was really difficult to get their attention, particularly after lunch or a break. I tried standing quietly at the front waiting for them to be quiet but this could take all lesson. So then I tried shouting at them, but the students just spoke more loudly over the top of me. In the end, I used a technique that I had used in my industry. I used to use a timer on the projector screen to count down how long applicants had to do a task, so I decided to do this with a countdown for two minutes to the start of the lesson. This actually worked, students seemed more interested in counting down with it than talking to each other. I would vary it in different lessons, anything from two minutes to twenty seconds. Not all of them were quiet when the timer ended, but at least the noise level was reduced so I could be heard and get started.

I then found it difficult to get them involved in the topic; they would often look at me blankly – it was really hard, it felt like wading through treacle to get it going. Then I read something in a book about starting the lesson with an easier task – reviewing what they have done before. This was better and it helped to get the students going in the lesson after which we could move on to something harder or new.

I decided to give out all the important information at the beginning of the lesson – such as assignment brief dates and so on, so that they make sure they come to the lesson on time. The trouble is if they are late or not paying attention I have to go through it all again and run out of time in the lesson.

I still feel nervous at the start of the lesson, especially with all the faces looking at me expectantly, but an experienced teacher who observed me recently told me that she still feels nervous even though she has been teaching for fifteen years. She said that she thinks it is a quality, shows that you take the lesson seriously, and it only lasts for a few moments. There is hope for me yet then!

Using reflection, Andy was able to identify the skills he needed to develop, and created strategies to do so. Nisha also developed her own strategies, but in particular used her colleagues as a valuable source for this.

CASE STUDY

Nisha: female, in her mid-30s

I have recently started a new job at my local university. It is where I gained my degree ten years ago. Since then I have been working at my local FE college, teaching on childcare courses. I felt ready for a change. The students I had worked with at the college were mainly

16–18 year-olds. The big difference for me is that I am now working with adult learners, many of whom are returning to learn after a long period away from education. This has meant I have had to rethink the teaching approaches that I use. I have also had difficulty believing in my own skills and knowledge; at times I have felt like a fraud. My students all seem to have more practical hands-on experience than me.

The team who teach on the course have been very supportive and have listened to my fears. They have been keen to offer me advice, which has been very practical. One of the team in particular has taken me for coffee and cake on a regular basis and is happy to answer questions about things that are worrying me and which I feel stupid asking. They have been very supportive peers, reassuring me that they felt like this when they first started. This has really helped my transition into the new teaching role.

One of my worries has been to do with tracking and monitoring student progress. I have not been used to doing this at the level required in the university. Over another cup of coffee it was suggested that for every new group I set them an initial writing task. This would help the students to start to develop their academic writing skills and give me the opportunity to learn about each student's strengths and possible issues. It also gave me the chance to mark work, which was formative and allowed me to note students' starting points and to begin tracking progress. A second worry was whether I would be able to support my learners emotionally. I had observed another tutor taking a very distressed student for a coffee and a chat. I did not think I would be able to do that. However, when I was confronted with this situation, I took the student away from the classroom, bought them a cup of coffee, listened to their story, offered what advice I could, but suggested that they talk to student services. I made the initial contact for them and went with them to the first appointment, just to show them the way and introduce them. This seemed to work well and the student stayed on the course and even sent me a card as a thank you.

One teaching strategy that has really helped me is the use of technology. This is something I am confident about and actually enjoy using. Two strategies in particular I have found helpful. Firstly I set a learning task each week which necessitates the students accessing the virtual learning environment. They have to find and read an article and then join in on an online discussion forum. Each week at the end of the session I show them where to find the article and how to post a message. This has enabled the entire group to become familiar with the use of technology. Secondly a lot of my students live some distance from the university and sometimes find it hard to make the journey just for a short tutorial. I have found using Skype very helpful. This has enabled me to hold a larger number of short tutorials for each student. The time that they save travelling to meet face to face has been used for the 'extra' tutorials. I was very conscious that for some students they prefer face to face, so I always gave the option. I have really enjoyed using my skills and knowledge in this way.

Chapter reflections

It has been interesting to look at these situations from the perspective of both a learner and a tutor. Have a look at the list of key themes that you made when reading these stories and see how it compares to ours.

Table 2.1 *Key themes*

Tutor themes	Learner themes
Know your learners	Lack of confidence
Motivating learners	Difficulties with motivation
Inclusive learning	External pressures
Strategies to ensure that all learners have the necessary skills to engage	Recognising existing knowledge and experience
Benefiting from colleagues as a community of practice	Benefiting from peers as a community of practice

These stories and their key themes are discussed and referred to in detail in the chapters that follow.

3 Motivation

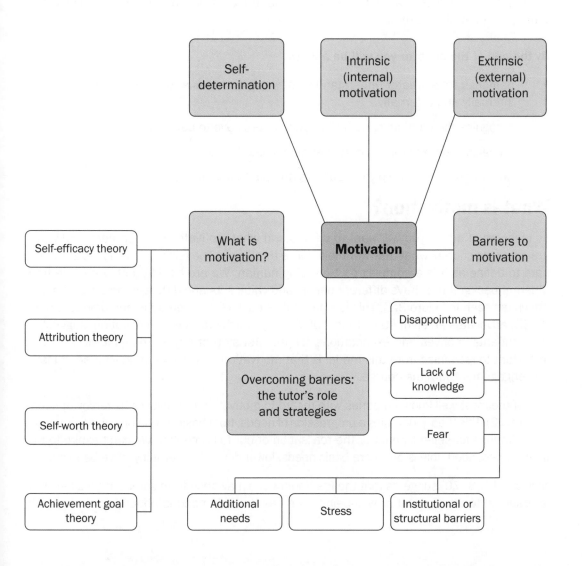

Chapter aims

'I can do it' or 'Am I too old to learn?'

The adult learners you will be teaching will have enrolled on your course for a number of probably quite complex reasons. These will not be as simple as the reasons that traditional students have. They will be both personal and professional. It may be that your adult learners will want to explore new knowledge for themselves, improve their self-esteem, self-worth and self-image, or are attending for professional reasons such as career enhancement. From our experience, what is evident is that the factors influencing motivation will be many and varied. Your learners may be highly motivated to persevere on their chosen course and indeed to succeed, or may be attending a course because they are required to do so and as such have low levels of motivation. This range of different motivating factors can be seen in Figure 3.1. In supporting adult learners to achieve their aims you will need to ensure that you have a good understanding of what motivates them, what the possible barriers are and how to help your learners overcome them.

By the end of the chapter you will be able to:

*   demonstrate a greater understanding of what motivates adult learners both internally and externally;

*   recognise the multiple roles that adult learners have to perform;

*   recognise some of the barriers that demotivate learners;

*   understand how to help your learners (to help themselves).

What is motivation?

As teachers of adults you will want to understand what motivates your learners – why they are doing the course; what they want to achieve by doing it. The term 'motivation' can be very hard to define as it is a complex part of being human. We are all different. We come from different backgrounds, have different beliefs and value sets and different factors that motivate us (as seen in Figure 3.1). This is what makes each of us interesting and unique. Gange (1998) advocates an eight-stage model of learning which starts with motivation, suggesting that students' motives and expectations are the first step of any learning journey. What is important to recognise from this model is that motivation is a key factor in your adult learners' engagement with the course.

One of the most well-known theories with regard to motivation is Maslow's hierarchy of needs (Figure 3.2). This theory identifies a progression of needs, from basic physiological requirements to aspirations for self-fulfilment or the realisation of our full potential. We can't aspire to this final, highest need unless our more basic needs, lower down the hierarchy, have been met.

Maslow (1908–70) suggests that the first four needs may arise from something we lack that is essential to our survival or well-being, whereas the final need is about personal growth.

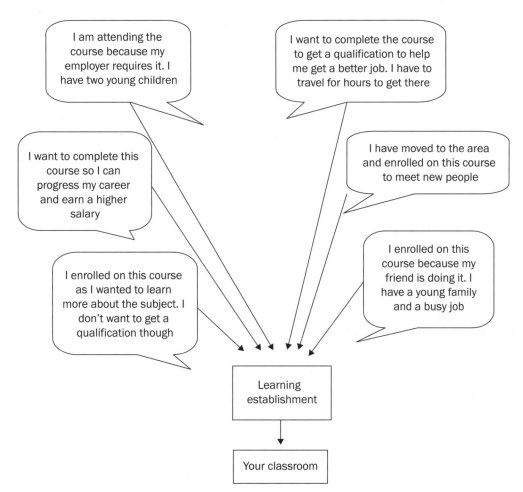

Figure 3.1 *Different motivations for learning*

This aspiration towards personal growth is what has motivated many of your adult learners to return to the classroom. Harkin et al. (2001) adapted and developed Maslow's model by paralleling and detailing how it links to an educational context. This can also be seen as a way for you to plan and reflect on how you prepare your sessions.

In terms of a classroom setting, basic needs can be seen as creating a welcoming and warm environment, where refreshment breaks are planned. Providing security can be seen as ensuring that there are 'group' rules that enable all learners to feel safe and be part of the group. Social needs could equate to learners' views and contributions being valued and their different learning styles being taken into account by the teacher. Students' need for building self-esteem can be met by providing suitable yet challenging learning tasks which support them to succeed. Finally, learners may be helped towards self-actualisation by the teacher providing them with the support they need to progress towards their goal, whether this is a qualification, a higher level course, or some other achievement (Figure 3.3).

Figure 3.2 *Maslow's hierarchy of needs*

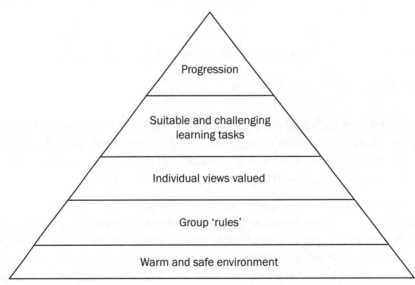

Figure 3.3 *Maslow's hierarchy of needs adapted for use in your classroom*

If you consider Maslow's theory from a student perspective, it may be, for example, that one of your learners has been at work all day and has not managed to get anything to eat. To compound the issue, facilities at your establishment may be limited or insufficient so they are unable to purchase a drink or some food when they arrive at college. Or perhaps they have arrived late because they have had to make emergency childcare arrangements or had difficulty parking. All of this 'discomfort' and hassle will mean that it will be difficult for that learner to clear their head in order to participate and engage in the lesson. A supportive teacher will be able to recognise this and help them to overcome their frustrations and focus on their learning. This may involve encouraging them to bring their own refreshments to class or not making them feel uncomfortable if they arrive late. We saw in James' story how the teacher formed good relationships with his learners at the start and how this proved to be very important when he later faced challenges. If James had not received this support from his teacher and his peers, he would very quickly have become demotivated.

Unlike Maslow, who identified observable factors that might impact on motivation, Wlodkowski (1999) described motivation as a hypothetical construct that cannot be observed. For your adult learners this may take the form of their need to achieve personal goals for enjoyment, rather than ones driven by their employer. Weiner (1992) claims that motivation can be viewed as a cycle. In other words, if your adult learners are motivated they will learn; if they are learning they are likely to achieve; and if they achieve they will be more motivated. We can observe how this has happened in Ben's story. But the work we are going to look at in more detail is that of Seifert (2004), who suggests that there are four main theories of motivation in an academic context: self-efficacy theory, attribution theory, self-worth theory and achievement goal theory.

Self-efficacy theory

The self-efficacy theory is related to how your adult learners make judgements about their own abilities to undertake learning to the level required by the course or training programme. Those who have plenty of self-confidence and who perceive themselves as capable of succeeding will be well on the road to achieving. On the other hand, learners who do not have strong self-efficacy may struggle with confidence and as a result may find achievement hard. Think about the learner who has a history of failure at school, resulting in low confidence. You will need to ensure you provide a variety of opportunities for them to succeed in both formative and summative assessed tasks.

Attribution theory

Attribution theory aims to identify why a particular outcome turned out the way it did. This is often associated with failing an assessment or not doing as well as the learner expected. The initial response may be driven by learner emotions and may impact on their future engagement with their learning. Let's imagine that one of your adult learners has done very well on their previous course which was at a lower level than the current one they are studying with you. The first summative piece of assessment on your course has been marked and, although your learner has passed, they are very disappointed at the mark awarded. You have noticed that they are arriving late for sessions and they are not sharing or joining in the discussion in the same way that they were at the start of the course. Weiner (1985) suggests that this is when the learner is *attributing* their 'failure' to some innate deficiency in themselves. He also argues that learners who believe failure has been as a result of internal uncontrollable factors may feel humiliation and shame, which in turn may lead to lack of engagement in future activities. This can be a common occurrence with adult learners. Sometimes they may respond emotionally, even, for example, sending you an angry e-mail as an expression of their disappointment in an assessment mark or frustration with the course or establishment. They may confront you as a teacher – seeing it as entirely your fault, maintaining that you did not teach them or explain things properly. Remember that your reaction in these situations can help to either motivate or further demotivate your learners, so you need to behave appropriately and professionally in your response. We discuss this further in Chapter 6 when we explore the uses of transactional analysis.

Self-worth theory

Self-worth can refer to a learner's view of their own sense of worth and dignity and this can be linked to their ability to do something well. A learner with a good sense of self-worth is likely to be able to achieve, whereas one with low or little self-worth may struggle to be motivated and therefore less likely to achieve.

Achievement goal theory

Finally, and equally relevant to adult learning, is what Seifert refers to as *achievement goal theory* (Seifert, 2004, p 142). Here he explores the concept that achievement of desired goals by learners is a key to motivation. This can be seen in the learners who have joined the course for the purpose, for example, of gaining qualifications to enhance their career prospects. It is important when you are thinking about and planning your sessions that you always bear in mind your learners' goals.

Self-determination

Deci and Ryan (1991) suggest that motivation is linked to self-determination. By this they mean that learners who want to develop and grow in a personal capacity must feel they have the freedom to do so without having to struggle against impossible constraints. In other words, they must have some sense of control over the direction their lives are taking. There are links here to Maslow's theory. In terms of your own practice this may mean that you need to think about areas such as the relevance of the material that you use, how you enable autonomous learning and ensure that the physical environment is comfortable, unthreatening and encourages some degree of learner choice. If you can achieve this your learners are more likely to be motivated in their studies and to be successful at the end of the course.

Figure 3.1 demonstrated that for most adult learners there are individual factors unique to them that motivated them to join a course. It is also important to recognise that there are a number of motivational factors that your learners may share.

Table 3.1 External Factors that may influence motivation

Factor	Influences on students' lives	Influences within the classroom and learning	Teacher actions
Personal beliefs and values: the principles that your individual learners hold in high regard	Culture, traditions, manners, the way they dress or behave. These values will guide them in their decision-making and in the way they lead their lives	How they approach or communicate with you, how they interact with their peers	Use materials and resources sensitive to cultural difference, consider how the language and terminology you use or what you do may offend your learners' beliefs or values
Family factors: influences and demands of families	Caring responsibilities for both younger and older family members. Expectations that family members have of the individual	Family history of engaging with education and achieving. There may be high expectations or challenges	Be sensitive to the demands of the individual. Recognise that families may undermine the confidence that the learner has, or they may encourage the learner to challenge your decisions regarding assessment

All of these can be factors in either intrinsic or extrinsic motivation (see pages 40–41).

Critical thinking activity

Having started to explore what might motivate your adult learners, you also need to reflect on your own personal motivating factors, beliefs and value sets.

» *Where have you gained your values from, for example family, friends, work? Which have had the most influence on you?*

» *How do you feel about your own learning journey? Which parts of that journey do you value the most?*

» *What are your values in areas such as race, gender, religion, language?*

» *Are you able to draw on sufficient knowledge and understanding in these areas to help you plan your own teaching and your own learning? Identify any gaps in your knowledge and understanding.*

Reflecting on these questions will help you to understand your own motivation and enable you to have empathy with your learners.

Intrinsic (internal) motivation

Wlodkowski (1999) suggests that it is human nature to be curious, and that adult learners use this curiosity to help them understand their own experiences. An example of this would be when you use your learners' experiences in your teaching, asking them to make the connections between theory and their own practice. Wlodkowski also suggests that intrinsic motivation – motivation that arises from within the learner rather than being driven by outside imperatives – can be governed by emotions. We can see this from the perspective of both the teacher and the learner. Look back at Nisha's story (page 30–31), where on starting a new job she was both worried and frightened about whether she could meet its demands. Ed had similar concerns about being a student on his course. Both Nisha and Ed, you will remember, were supported in their journeys by their peers.

Your learners may view their adult learning experience as a welcome personal challenge. This could be an intellectual challenge; a challenge in terms of risk taking; a challenge in doing something new or in meeting new people; or a challenge in learning a new skill. Or they may be motivated as a result of their family history, having seen other family members return to learning and recognising that it may 'open doors'.

Intrinsic motivation may also take the form of a desire to make up for previous lost opportunities. Perhaps the school curriculum was not 'right' for them or they were excluded from education. Or they may wish to break a cycle of poor educational achievement by supporting their own children. Maxted (1999) suggests that family life is the foundation for learning for children and that 85 per cent of their learning takes place in the home. Or perhaps the adult learner is driven simply by the need to prove to themselves and others that they can 'do it'. The National Adult Learning Survey (2010), for example, found that 49 per cent of respondents entered learning in order to develop new skills and 32 per cent entered in order to boost their self-confidence.

Critical thinking activity

» *You have a new group of learners on your course. They are made up of a mix of ages and experiences, but within the group you have a number of adult learners. Rather than making assumptions about their motivation to return to learn, how would you set about finding out why they are on the course?*

» *Thinking about your current classes, try to identify those of your learners with strong intrinsic motivations.*

» *Have they shared their motivations with you or have you encouraged them to do so?*

» *How might you use this knowledge in teaching and supporting them within your class?*

Gathering information of this sort will help you to get to know your learners and it will help them get to know one another. Developing good relationships with and between your learners from the outset can be another important way to encourage and sustain their motivation. If coming to college feels comfortable, and the social aspects of learning are valued and reinforced, demotivators such as anxiety and stress are unlikely to build up and 'turn off' learners' enthusiasm. This is explored further in Chapter 6.

Internal motivation may also be affected by your learner's innate ability or intelligence – usually manifested in their ability to engage with problem solving, and to some extent determined by their prior experiences and cultural references. Howard Gardiner's (1983) work on multiple intelligences suggests that intelligence is not a single entity, nor is it a hierarchical system of abilities. Rather it is composed of a number of different 'intelligences' which are independent of each other. It is these intelligences that dictate individual learners' preferred learning styles. This is a useful concept to bear in mind when you are planning lessons as it can help you to devise activities that will meet the sometimes disparate needs of all your learners.

Extrinsic (external) motivation

Many of your learners may be motivated not by an intrinsic, internal drive, but by external pressures such as the need to develop new skills and knowledge, or to gain qualifications in order to further their career development, or indeed to train to maintain the employment they may already have. We refer to these external drivers as 'extrinsic motivation'. This type of motivation can spring from a work-based appraisal system, where need has been identified for Further Education and training that can be transferred back into the workplace. In this case your learners will have been 'sent' on your course. The National Adult Learning Survey (2010) describes these learners as 'means-to-enders' and states that they are only interested in undertaking the course if there is a tangible reward at the end, such as a qualification or a greater salary. The learners who enter your classroom with this instrumental end in mind may present you with different problems in terms of motivation. For example, they may feel resentment at having to attend, or they may believe that there is nothing you can usefully teach them. If, on the other hand, they are re-entering learning to improve their chances of gaining employment, as seen in Figure 3.1, they may be driven by the need to enhance the family income, to keep up with others in their workplace, or to avoid the risk of redundancy. This type of 'means-to-ender' may well resent the need to be in class at all (Muller and Louw, 2004).

Table 3.2 presents a categorised summary of types of adult learners and is based on the National Adult Learning Survey (2010). Whilst this is not a definitive list, it provides a useful 'thumbnail' sketch of the range of learners you may encounter, their backgrounds, motivations and the possible barriers to learning that they may need to overcome.

Table 3.2 Types of learners and their motivation (based on National Adult Learning Survey, 2010)

Type of learner	Motivation	Barriers
Pro-learning go-getters: Have spent a number of years in full-time education. Are likely to be highly qualified and higher earners	• See learning as an investment • Desire to improve skills and knowledge • Potential for improving job prospects and satisfaction	• Engagement at all cost • Stress levels • Unrealistic expectations
Pro-learning planners: Likely to be 40 and under and to have caring responsibilities – young families. Well educated and higher earners	• See learning as an investment in the future • Recognition of the positive benefits of learning	• Availability of courses • Flexibility of delivery • Time poor
Distracted advocates: Well-educated higher learners who may be willing to return to study	• Value learning • Need to keep up to date to stay on top in the job market • To improve performance • To gain promotion	• Not willing to give up free time – after-work commitments • Find it hard to find free time
Fear of failure: Mainly female with poor qualifications and unlikely to be in employment. Poor experience of education	• To build confidence, self-worth • To help children with learning	• Time • Availability of courses • Worry about keeping up with others
Means-to-enders: Few or no qualifications. Unlikely to be in employment. Likely to have left full-time education at 16	• To build confidence and self-worth • To improve employment prospects	• View learning as only worthwhile if there is a qualification at the end • Lack of confidence • Do not believe skills can be transferred
Too old to learn: Likely to be over 70 and with few qualifications	• View learning as a pleasurable activity • To help and support grandchildren • Not wanting to be 'left behind'	• Learning not for us • Too old and disinterested • Prefer to spend time on 'what they want'

Critical thinking activity

» *Reflecting on Table 3.2, can you identify any of these characteristics in the learners that you teach?*

» *Do you recognise the types of barriers illustrated? You may identify other barriers as you reflect on your own experiences in the classroom.*

» *Consider ways to break down those barriers.*

Barriers to motivation

The barriers that learners face are rarely insurmountable. In this section we will explore some of the more common barriers to learning that adult returners may experience. There are a number that can be described as traditional barriers, such as family commitments, financial difficulties or accessibility issues (Davies et al., 2002). Others may include institutional barriers such as policies and procedures, and differing perceptions and expectations between the learner and the institution. Some of these factors will be beyond your control and beyond that of your learners. However, you may be able to address others such as those to do with the institutional or classroom environment.

Disappointment

Your learners will come to your classroom with differing notions and expectations with regard to how a classroom should be or how they should be taught. For example, it may be that they believed their return to learning would be easy and the tasks well within their capability, and then discover that this is not the case. Or they may have expected larger classes, in which they could avoid drawing notice to themselves; or smaller classes in which they could secure a great deal of one-to-one help and attention from the teacher. Finding that the reality does not meet with their expectations can create an initial and potentially damaging barrier to their learning. They may also have preconceived ideas about the 'what', 'why' and 'how' of learning and teaching. Crowder and Pupnin (1995) recognised that a learner's expectation of a learning exercise will determine how motivated they might be in pursuing that activity. Therefore, it is always worthwhile taking some time to ask adult learners about their expectations and preconceived ideas as part of finding out what they hope to gain from their return to learning. The opportunity to talk through such issues can go a long way towards preventing barriers of resentment and disappointment arising.

Lack of knowledge

Your learners may also be conscious of, or fear, a lack of essential knowledge. This can be summarised as the idea that, *There's something I ought to know, and everyone else will know it, but I don't know what it is*. It is important to remember that many of them will not have been in a formal learning situation for number of years and may be worried about returning to learn and all that this might entail, including for example the use of technology. Remember Hadas' story. She was anxious about the use technology, and although she was able to overcome this when she was reassured by the tutor demonstrating and using it, for others anxiety about 'inadequacies' of this sort can constitute a serious barrier to learning.

Fear

In the context of adult learning, fear can take many forms. This may be fear of non-completion (Powell, 2008) or fear of failure (as expressed by Ed), or a fear of being too old to learn. Or it may be the fear of inadequate knowledge as discussed above. Fear is perhaps the greatest of all barriers to learning, as it gives the learner a sense of being 'unsafe' in all sorts of ways; and, as we have seen from Maslow's hierarchy of needs, if their need for a sense of safety is not met, the individual is unable to aspire to any higher fulfilment such as learning.

Additional needs

Other barriers to motivation may include factors that necessitate additional support, such as a recognised disability of some kind. Your educational establishment's policies and procedures, including student support services, should provide both support and guidance in order for these potential barriers to be overcome. We discuss how you can do this in Chapter 6.

Stress

Another factor that may affect motivation is stress. A number of authors (for example Powell, 2008; Wlodkowski, 1999; Seifert, 2004) all indicate that stress may have an impact on learners' memory and this in turn may affect motivation. The more stressed a learner becomes the more difficult it can be for them to stay focused, motivated and engaged in their learning. Your adult learners may manifest this stress in a number of ways. You may be bombarded with e-mails; you may find they are asking the same questions time and again; or perhaps they want to 'get started' on assessment activities before they are ready or before all of the relevant teaching has taken place; or they may be struggling to access materials on the virtual learning environments. All of these types of stress indicators, if recognised, can begin to be addressed if the source of stress is related to the learning process or institution. However, if the stress arises from the learner's external circumstances (their life outside college), you may need to direct them to student support services for advice or specialist help such as counselling.

Institutional or structural barriers

Other barriers to motivation may include institutional or structural ones, which are often determined by the establishment's policies and procedures. Some of these barriers may well start from the moment your prospective adult learner contacts the establishment: do the advice and guidance team know how to respond to the particular requirement and questions that your learners might ask? Other potential barriers can be the lack of choice of course; poor provision; limited resources available outside normal teaching hours; or even tutors who have not understood or developed the skills needed to work with adult learners. Another may be the timing of sessions. Davies et al. (2002) identified that the way in which a course was timetabled and the availability of resources and access to support services was a disincentive for some adult learners already struggling to cope with the demands of studying as well as managing life outside education. All of these examples are beyond your learners' control and could impact greatly on their motivation. Recognising the potential impact of these barriers will help you to better meet your learners' needs.

Overcoming barriers: the tutor's role and strategies

Stipek (2001) suggests that when learners are intrinsically motivated they tend to:

*   prefer challenges in learning rather than 'easy' work which may not enhance either skills or knowledge;

*   take responsibility for their learning and in doing so work independently;

*   use an internal mechanism to inform their personal success (or indeed failure).

These points can provide a framework from which to develop the strategies that you might use in order to help your adult learners. For example, you will need to set challenging work and, in doing so, allow your adult learners the opportunity for both independent study and for making use of their life experiences.

It is important to recognise that you have a key role in helping your adult learners to stay motivated. This role may challenge the way in which you prepare and teach your sessions. A good starting point in understanding this challenge will be for you to expect that all of your adult learners are more than capable of learning. You will also need to believe that they can be successful in their studies, that they see value in their learning and, above all, that they feel supported and safe. Consider, for example, how Andy discovered new ways to engage his learners and build their confidence. Creating a supportive learning environment involves things such as encouraging risk taking and planning plenty of opportunities for formative feedback both from you as a tutor and from learners, peer to peer. You will remember from Ed's story that peer feedback was a strategy he found particularly helpful. Most importantly of all, of course, is that you show care and respect for your learners.

Here are some useful strategies that you might like to try.

*   Know your learners' starting point: what have they studied before, at what level and how well did they do? Also note *when* they last studied. Knowing these things will enable you to plan your initial sessions based on your learners' needs. You may consider carrying out a formative assessment task near the start of the course. The results of this may help you to diagnose learning needs, choose what topic or skill to cover next, and support them to achieve (Ecclestone, 1996). Remember that you should use your student support services to help you with learners who have a specific learning difficulty.

*   Be empathetic to your learners' home situations. Take time to listen, but also ensure you direct your learners to the relevant support.

- Make your sessions purposeful; ensure you incorporate students' interests; build on their wealth of life experiences and knowledge. Recognise and value these experiences and draw on them to support your teaching. Remember that you might not know all the answers and that it is fine, and indeed productive, as it allows you to draw on your learners' experiences and expertise. This has the added benefit of making learners feel valued and respected for who they are and where they have come from;

- Be aware of your choice of language. Try and communicate key messages and information as flexibly as possible. Be positive and affirming rather than negative and coercive. For example, avoid starting a session with something along the lines of *I know this is boring, but we have to cover it.* You can't get much more demotivating than that.

- Be aware of how you use your body language: give good eye contact and be open to your learners' needs. Try and ensure you observe your learners' body language too. It may give you clues as to how they are engaging (see Chapter 6).

- Work *with* your learners to ensure they are not simply passive recipients. Again this links back to using their skills, experiences and knowledge.

- Use technology such as podcasts, online discussion forums and Skype tutorials as appropriate to maximise one-to-one and group contact (see Chapter 5).

- Autonomy: ensure you give your adult learners a voice and opportunities for self-reflection and evaluation. This will make them feel valued and motivated.

In Chapter 4 we discuss in more detail a whole range of strategies that will help you to support your adult learners. However, we strongly believe that it is the way in which you engage and work with your learners that has the strongest influence on their motivation, engagement and ultimate success. The reality of formal study, and especially part-time study, is that individual teachers can make or break a learner's experience. As the time spent in the classroom will be very limited, it is paramount that you get things right. The teacher is essential to the creation of the supportive social and learning environment of the classroom. McGiveney captures this perfectly:

> We can talk till the cows come home about the vital importance of guidance but we are seriously in error if we do not acknowledge the pivotal guidance role of the tutor for the part- time learner. For many the teacher is the guidance system.
>
> (McGiveney, 1996, p 135)

Your adult learners may well be studying full-time rather than part-time, but McGiveney's words still apply.

Chapter reflections

This chapter has discussed what we mean by 'motivation' and what might motivate your adult learners to return to learning. It has also explored factors that might influence both intrinsic and extrinsic motivation. One of the key themes that emerges when trying to explore and understand motivation is recognising the relevance of learners' experiences, not only to their motivation but also to the way in which you plan your teaching. Finally we have discussed and explored issues with regard to motivational barriers to learning and how these might be overcome.

In summary, this chapter argues the need for a framework that encourages motivation. Wlodkowski and Ginsberg (1995, p 8) provide such a framework of 'conditions' which support learner motivation: 'establishing inclusion, developing attitude, enhancing meaning and engendering competence'. These will help to create an atmosphere and environment where everyone feels respected, and where your own and your learners' experiences are drawn upon to support the teaching and learning, and to provide challenge, rigour and encouragement.

Taking it further

If you would like to find out more about theories of motivation and how these might impact on your adult learners you may find Howard Gardiner's (1998) book on multiple intelligences and Harkin et al.'s (2001) work on teaching young adults useful. Both are shown in the references section below.

References

Crowder, N, and Pupynin, K (1995) *Understanding Learner Motivation*. Nottingham: DfEE.

Davies, P, Osborne, M and Williams, J (2002) *For Me or Not for Me? That is the Question: A Study of Students' Decision Making and Higher Education*. Norwich: Her Majesty's Stationery Office.

Deci, E and Ryan, M (1991) Motivation and Education: The Self-Determination Perspective. *The Educational Psychologist*, 26: 325–46.

Ecclestone, K (1996) *How to Assess the Vocational Curriculum*. London: Kogan Page.

Gange, R (1998) *Principles of Instructional Design*. New York: Holt, Rinehart and Winston.

Gardiner, H (1983) *Frames of Mind: Theory of Multiple Intelligences*. New York: Basic Books.

Ghaye, T (2011) *Teaching and Learning through Reflective Practice*. Abingdon: Routledge.

Goleman, D (1996) *Emotional Intelligence*. London: Bloomsbury.

Harkin, J, Turner, G and Dawn, T (2001) *Teaching Young Adults*. London: Routledge Falmer.

Maslow, A (1987) *Motivation and Personality*. New York: Harper and Row.

Maxted, P (1999) *Understanding Barriers to Learning*. Exmouth: Campaign for Learning.

McGiveney, V (1996) *Staying or Leaving the Course: Non-Completion and Retention of Mature Students in Further and Higher Education*. Leicester: NIACE.

Muller, F, Louw, J (2004) Learning Environment, Motivation and Interest: Perspectives on Self-Determination Theory. *South African Journal of Psychology*, 25: 54–67.

National Adult Learning Survey (2010) Research Paper 63. London: Department for Business Innovation and Skills.

Powell, S (2008) *Returning to Study for a Research Degree*. Maidenhead: Open University Press.

Seifert, T (2004) Understanding Student Motivation. *Educational Research*, 46 (2): 137–49.

Stipek, D (2001) *Motivation to Learn: Integrating Theory and Practice.* Boston: Pearson Alynn and Bacon.

Weiner, B (1985) in Seifert, T (2004) *Understanding Student Motivation.* Educational Research, 46 (2): 137–49.

Weiner, B (1992) *Human Motivation: Metaphors, Theories and Research.* California: Sage

Wlodkowski, R and Ginsberg, M (1995) *Diversity and Motivation: Culturally Responsive Teaching.* San Fransisco: Jossey-Bass.

Wlodkowski, R (1999) *Enhancing Adult Motivation to Learn.* San Francisco: Jossey-Bass.

4 The practicalities of teaching adult learners

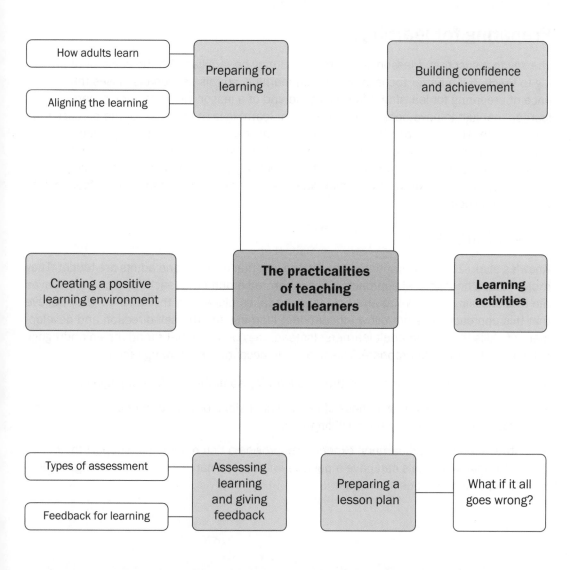

Chapter aims

This chapter explores the essentials and practicalities of teaching adults. It examines the importance of preparation and of linking learning activities with learning objectives to create a positive and active environment. It also discusses how to build learners' confidence through planning, assessment and the use of supportive feedback.

By the end of the chapter you will be able to:

*   recognise how adults learn;

*   identify the need to plan for learning;

*   suggest a variety of activities that are appropriate for adult learners;

*   recognise how to build the confidence of adult learners;

*   identify the expectations of adult learners.

Preparing for learning

The key to a successful lesson is planning. You may be familiar with the concept of preparing to teach, but a better focus is on student learning, so this section discusses the importance of preparing for learning. After all, at the end of a lesson we want our learners to have learned, not just to have been taught. If student learning is at the heart of the process then we can plan what we want them to learn, design lessons and create an environment to enable them to learn, assess whether they have learned, and make opportunities for them to reflect on or apply their learning. To do this effectively you need to understand the process of adult learning and know how to plan lessons, assess learners and provide feedback to develop and support them.

How adults learn

Knowles et al. (2011) differentiate between the way that children and adults are taught. They explain that a pedagogical approach which is centred around the teaching of children leaves the responsibility about what and how learning takes place with the teacher. They believe that this approach does not allow independent learning and the self-direction and development of skills required in adult learners. Instead, they propose that for adults an andragogical approach is more appropriate. This takes into account the following factors:

*   the adult's need to know why they are learning something before engaging in it;

*   that adults have an awareness of being responsible for their own decisions and can resist others imposing their will on them;

*   the fact that adult learners' experiences provide a rich resource to support their learning. Whilst this can have a positive influence, it can also inhibit learning if they have had difficulties in the past;

- adult learners often show a greater readiness to learn than younger learners if their learning is relevant to their own developmental stage;

- adults are more receptive to learning when it is presented in context with real-life situations;

- although still motivated by external factors, adults tend to be more internally motivated.

If we are able to recognise the process of learning from an adult perspective then we are more likely to be able to design their learning experiences to ensure that they have the best opportunity to learn. However, we also have to remember that all learners are individuals who bring to the class their own abilities, personalities, prior knowledge, experience and motivation.

Critical thinking activity

Look back at the student stories of Ed, James, Mateusz, Hadas and Ben in Chapter 2.

» Would you say that they were ready to learn?

» If so, identify how this was manifested at the start of the course and later on.

» In particular, what was it that engaged Mateusz in his course?

Aligning the learning

You may be teaching on a short one-day course or a long course lasting several years. It doesn't matter how long or short the course is, it will have course outcomes – this will be stipulated by the awarding body and defines the knowledge, understanding, skills, qualities and attributes that a successful learner will be able to demonstrate by the end of the course. These will often be written in fairly general terms. Long courses are usually then divided into a number of modules, and you may be teaching on one or more modules of a course. Each module will also have outcomes that state the knowledge, understanding, skills, qualities and attributes that learners will be able to demonstrate at the end of that module. These outcomes will be similar to the course learning outcomes, but will be more specifically related to the module. As long as there is a similarity between the course and module outcomes, they can be said to be 'aligned'. When designing a lesson, you will need to establish what you want the learners to achieve, and therefore you need to define learning objectives or outcomes for that lesson (or in some cases a series of lessons). These learning outcomes should also relate to the outcomes for the module, but they are specifically focused on learner achievement over a shorter time period. If the lesson outcomes relate to the module outcomes, the lesson is then aligned with *both* the module and course outcomes. Once you have established the lesson outcomes, you need to decide how you can measure the learning in that lesson. So the activities and tasks that you choose should be designed to measure whether the students have learned what you intended them to learn.

Table 4.1 An example of alignment of learning outcomes

Course learning outcome	Module learning outcomes	Lesson learning outcomes	Lesson activities and assessment
Undertake research into educational practices and policies and make recommendations to improve learning experiences	Undertake research using primary sources, ensuring that this is done appropriately and ethically	Identify the process of research State how research is undertaken ethically	Trial and discuss three different research methods Discuss ethical issues arising in research
	Using relevant theory, justify your choice of research methods	Identify the strengths and limitations of three research methods	In groups, using research textbooks, identify strengths and weaknesses of three given methods and share with the class
	Analyse your own findings, and make suitable judgements which may improve practice	Undertake analysis of research findings Identify how learning experiences can be improved as a result of the research	Discuss research findings with a peer and suggest two ways that practice can be improved
	Undertake a self-critical evaluation of your work identifying action points to improve practical research skills	Explain the purpose of self-evaluation Identify how self-evaluation can lead to improvement in technique	Prepare a pro forma for self-evaluation Undertake the evaluation and identify three action points

By using this approach, you can ensure that your learners have a cohesive experience and can see the relevance of their lessons and activities to their course. This approach can be seen to support the andragogical model of learning as described by Knowles et al. (2011, p 181) who state that *engaging adults as collaborative partners for learning satisfies their need to know as well as appeals to their self-concept as independent learners*. Aligning the learning in this way and sharing it with the adult learners can therefore enable them to participate more fully in the process as they see the immediate relevance and importance. We can see this in Mateusz's story where he reflects that once lessons showed that they had a purpose, his engagement and attendance improved. However, it is a shame that this did not happen until week four as some learners may have stopped attending by then. Harman and McDowell (2011) also explain that constructively aligning learning outcomes can aid objectivity in the assessment of student work. It can also be a useful mechanism to ensure that there is limited repetition between different teachers on a course or module. This is effectively done by preparing a programme of learning or a 'scheme of work'.

While it is important to align the course and modules with lessons activities, it is crucial to avoid both adopting a mechanistic approach and teaching to assessment. Fallows and Chandramohan (2001) discuss the dangers of students focusing on assessment criteria to the exclusion of other aspects of a course where the assessment becomes the main focus of the lessons. Whilst assessment is essential to the learning process, it should not dominate it.

Learning activities

As discussed above, the activities need to relate to what you want the students to learn in the lesson. If you want them to be able to analyse a poem, then the activities in the lesson need to build up to this skill. If you want them to be able to perform a certain practical task, you will not be able to assess this unless they actually demonstrate it. Therefore, the objectives of your lesson will be linked to the activities that the learners will do. We saw how this links together in Table 4.1.

There are many learning activities that you can incorporate into your lessons – your choice of these will depend on your subject, the time you have and your resources.

Critical thinking activity

» Consider the learning activities in Table 4.2 below. Assess whether you think each would be suitable for use with adult learners.

Table 4.2 Examples of learning activities (continued overleaf)

Activity	Can be useful for assessing	How it could be used	Would this be suitable for adults? Yes/no
Role play	How a student would behave in a certain situation	To bring some reality into a subject, to assess how learners interact and behave in a situation. Scenarios will need to be pre-prepared and may need to include scripts depending on the learners participating	

Activity	Can be useful for assessing	How it could be used	Would this be suitable for adults? Yes/no
Simulations	How a student would behave and respond in a certain situation	Introduces a greater depth of realism than a role play, can be useful to experience situations that cannot be experienced in normal situations	
Worksheets	Learner achievement in a topic	To assess the learning of a concept or completion of questions by completing pre-prepared worksheets	
Discussion	Social interaction, development of ideas, speaking and listening skills	To develop ideas from an initial concept, to work out how to design or plan a practical task	
Debate	Formulation of a critical argument, expressing a point clearly	To explore different views in a given topic

Can be used to explore a contentious topic | |
| Group work | Collective student knowledge about a topic | To share and develop ideas, to create an artefact or presentation | |
| Questions and answers | To ascertain previous learning, to determine learning achieved in a lesson | Can be verbal personalised questions to a class; verbal questions to a group following an activity; written tasks followed by verbal questions to share answers with the class | |
| Presentation | Knowledge of a topic, communication skills

Ability to answer questions on the topic | To bring together ideas on a topic covered in a lesson or series of lessons. To present knowledge of a subject learned outside a lesson | |

Activity	Can be useful for assessing	How it could be used	Would this be suitable for adults? Yes/no
Gapped handouts	Identification of missing text to consolidate knowledge	Learning languages, sciences, scripts	
Quiz	To determine knowledge of a subject	At the end of a lesson or module to check learning in a fun and informal way	
Word searches and crosswords	To determine knowledge of a subject	A question is set and the learner needs to find the answer in the word search or work out the answer to fit in the crossword grid. Can be used in any subject, eg sciences, languages. Will only determine low-level learning	
Demonstration	To determine learner's ability to perform a task	Can be used in any subject where a practical skill is to be learned	
Stories	To assess communication skills, creativity	Can be used in many subjects, particularly humanities where students create and develop stories on a given topic either in a group or individually	
Games	To assess knowledge and learning of a subject	Many games such as bingo, dominoes and card games can be adapted to test learners' knowledge of a range of topics. They can be pitched at different levels of learning	

Table 4.2 gives examples of a variety of learning activities and how they can be used. When used effectively, they will engage learners who will then enjoy participating in their lessons. It is important to prepare and practise these activities and develop skills to manage them in the classroom. However, do not overdo it and pack the lesson full of activities otherwise your learners will become exhausted and will not be able to consolidate the learning if they are rushed on too soon. It is important to ensure that the activities you plan are appropriate for the learners you are teaching. It would be advisable to get more information and guidance about the activities you are planning to use. There are websites that can be used to prepare worksheets, crosswords and word searches.

In relation to the critical thinking activity and Table 4.2, which of these would be suitable for adult learners? Adult learners may not want to participate in activities that they consider too childish but, if designed carefully, *all* of the activities in the table can be used in a creative and educational way. However, as discussed earlier, you will need to explain the relevance of them to your learners.

Critical thinking activity

» *Using Table 4.2, find new lesson activities that you could use in your teaching and identify how effectively they will engage your learners and support their learning.*

Preparing a lesson plan

If you are planning a long car journey or a holiday, it is likely that you will have a map or plan to ensure that you get to your destination or have a good holiday. Similarly, if you want to teach a good lesson and you want your learners to have a valuable learning experience, this also needs planning. Your plan should identify:

• what you want to achieve in the lesson (lesson aim);

• what you want the learners to achieve (learning or lesson objectives/outcomes);

• what the learners will do (activities);

• how you will know the learners have learned (assessment strategies);

• how you will ensure that the learners know they have learned and how they can develop their learning further (feedback).

A successful lesson does not happen by luck. You will need to think about how long each stage of the lesson will take. It is often easiest to work backwards. Identify how long the lesson is due to last and then work out how long your introduction and conclusion should last. Then you will know how long you have left in the lesson. This can be divided into smaller timeframes and you can allocate different amounts of time for each activity and assessment. Remember to include time to feed back to learners. The most successful lesson will engage your learners quickly, so ensure that they are doing some form of activity or discussion within the first 10–15 minutes of the lesson. If you look at the difficulties Andy had in starting a lesson, he found that an easy task early in the lesson got the learners going and engaged them in the session before moving onto harder or more complex issues. This is a good example of developing a topic.

A good lesson will be the result of a well-structured, aligned plan that identifies what the learning outcomes are, how the learners will achieve these and how they will be assessed to measure their achievement. Wallace (2011) makes a clear point that every lesson should be the result of a developmental planning process with a formalised lesson plan. She argues that by having a formal plan for each lesson, teachers can give more thought to the logical sequence of learning, the timing for the various stages and the pace of the lesson, and they will be able to consider and identify suitable activities to assess learning. Therefore, it can be argued that alignment of learning outcomes, activities and assessment can only be achieved through a formal planning process.

What if it all goes wrong?

All teachers, even the most experienced, will have times when things go wrong. This may be due to failure of equipment, activities in the lesson that did not work as intended, learners who did not engage in the activities, learners who did not understand what to do, or learners who did not achieve what was intended. When this happens, do not panic. You will need to think on your feet and improvise an alternative activity if the equipment fails. The following list contains some handy tips on what you can do if things go wrong.

- If the activities did not work as intended, you can be honest with the learners and explain what was planned – you may need to adapt what they were going to do and this may even result in a better strategy than the original one.

- If the learners do not appear to understand, ask them questions to ascertain whether they do or not, and be prepared to explain the activity in a different way. Sometimes getting one learner to explain it to others (assuming they have understood it correctly) can be helpful as they put it in their own words which their peers may be able to grasp better.

- When you are in a situation where an activity is simply not working, despite trying alternative ways, it would be better to end it. You could use the opportunity to reflect with the learners on why it did not work and what you were trying to achieve. You can revise previous lessons instead and get feedback from learners about their learning and progress. In other words, use the time in other ways rather than persisting with something that is going nowhere.

Creating a positive learning environment

A productive and suitable environment is needed in order for learning to take place. It may not be possible for you to have the ideal learning environment with all the resources and equipment you might need at your disposal, but you can maximise the environment and facilities that you have. There are some simple basic rules for this.

- Room layout: ensure that you can see all the learners and they can see you, your display or presentation and any demonstrations that you may do. Interaction with peers is an effective way of learning and is best achieved by arranging the room in a horseshoe layout or in groups. We saw in James' story how a horseshoe layout helped him to interact with his younger peers and start to build relationships which became very important to him later. Ideally students will not have their backs to each other, particularly when you want them to engage in a discussion. You may think that you need to control the class and believe that an arrangement of tables in rows is the best way to do this, but this will actually create barriers between you and the learners and allows them to 'hide' behind people in front. It can also obstruct their view of your presentation or demonstration. This layout can evoke fear in adults relating to their school experiences and can result in a negative learning environment, whereas a horseshoe format enables them to talk to their peers, which may help to alleviate fears and concerns.

- A clear working space: some learners have a tendency to leave their bags on the tables during the lesson. It is a good idea to discourage this as it can create a barrier between you and the learner and it is a distraction. A good rule would be to have bags stowed away under desks. This will be very important when you are doing practical activities.

- Ground rules: an effective technique for establishing a positive learning environment is agreeing ground rules with learners at the beginning of a course, term or module. This would include no talking over each other, respecting the viewpoints of others, punctuality and not using mobile phones. Your stance on the use of mobile phones in class will depend on you and your specific learners. Ideally, they should be put away and turned off. However, you may have some learners who need to be contactable, in which case phones should be switched to silent with the learner leaving the room if they need to take a call. This is often the case with adults who may need to be contactable by their children's school or carers. However, this should be an exception rather than regular practice as it disturbs not only the learner, but you and the other learners too. Other ground rules may also be appropriate and will depend on the age and profile of your learners and the subject that you are teaching.

Assessing learning and giving feedback

Assessment is not a remote, disconnected, linear quality assurance process (Harman and McDowell, 2011), it is an integral part of the learning to enable learners to receive feedback on their progress in order that they can recognise their strengths and work on areas that need to be developed. Formative assessment provides feedback to the student within the context of the assessment parameters but in such a way that it allows them to develop their skills, learn from their experience, build relationships with their tutors and prepare for a final assessment. This is sometimes referred to as 'assessment for learning'. Summative assessment involves judging learner achievement against a determined set of criteria (the assessment learning outcomes). This is sometimes referred to as 'assessment of learning'.

Types of assessment

Initial assessment

Initial assessment usually happens at the beginning of a course where the teaching team get to know the learners. During this stage you will need to establish students' previous knowledge and experience, their confidence, their character types – are they likely to be quiet or vocal in the lessons, and what particular needs or additional support requirements might they have? The importance of getting to know your learners is discussed further in Chapter 6 where we explore how to build relationships.

Initial assessment does not occur only at the start of a course. It still has a role at the beginning of a module or even a lesson to determine learners' previous knowledge or experience. If you have learners who already know or have experience in the topic, they are a valuable resource as you can use their knowledge in the lesson by asking them to explain it, or to support other learners to consolidate their knowledge. We saw how Nisha developed initial assessments when she started each group she taught. This gave her an opportunity to assess the learners' academic writing skills and to give formative feedback that would help them with these skills. It was also an opportunity for Nisha to obtain some feedback from her peers about the level of writing that would be expected as she was new to teaching at a Higher Education level.

Formative assessment

Formative assessment occurs in many ways and will be linked to the activities that the learners are doing in the lesson. Questions asked in the class are a common way of assessing learner understanding of a topic. However, it requires skill to use questioning effectively. It is not uncommon for teachers to ask questions of a whole class – in doing so responses tend to come only from the most confident or outspoken learners. It allows learners not to participate in the lesson if they know they do not have to answer. A useful technique is to ask the question of the whole class, give them all a moment to formulate a response and then ask a particular learner for an answer. In this way teachers are able to ensure all learners are participating, they can actively involve the quieter individuals, and they can differentiate the questioning by asking less-confident learners straightforward questions and more-confident learners more complex questions. It is important to explain the answers to the questions posed, even if they have been answered competently by a learner, in case some learners did not hear or did not understand the response. To develop questioning techniques further, secondary or subsidiary questions can be asked to explore the topic in more depth. If a learner is struggling to answer a question they should not be made to feel uncomfortable as they will disengage in the situation and may lose confidence in themselves. A useful strategy is to ask if anyone can help them out. If Debbie had used targeted questioning in her lessons, she could have ensured that the two chatty students were involved in the lesson more and would not have had the opportunity to talk to each other.

Hadas discussed how important formative feedback was for her to develop confidence in her own ability, both in terms of the subject and her use of technology. In her example, the tutor gave regular feedback on small tasks to support her learning and also set a requirement for it to be submitted to the website, enabling the learners to become familiar with this technology. As part of scaffolding this learning, the tutor demonstrated to the learners how to do this in the lessons. This helps the adult learner to feel supported in the building of their skills and confidence.

Formative assessment can also be undertaken by reviewing assignment proposals and plans and giving feedback on these to help the learners develop their ideas. We have seen that a number of students have found this helpful. Ed has identified how giving feedback to a peer made him feel more confident despite being reticent at first. On reflection, he may have benefited from this confidence boost before week seven. Worksheets and written or drawing tasks are ideal opportunities to assess learner achievement in lessons and provide the tutor with a chance to give personalised individual feedback. Practical activities should be assessed to determine learner performance and behaviour which may indicate their understanding. This can also be accompanied by verbal questioning to establish the learners' reasons for their actions. Again, this provides another opportunity to give personalised feedback to the learners.

Critical thinking activity

» *Identify the range of opportunities that you could use to informally assess your learners to determine their learning rather than your teaching.*

The importance of formative assessment cannot be overestimated. As Boud (2000, p 152) states, *we need to introduce high quality formative assessment practices because it is engagement with these practices which provides a secure foundation for lifelong learning and contributes directly to a learning society.* Boud explains that formative assessment is the key to learning as it enables teachers and learners to check their understanding and performance in a subject and to then make changes to correct or improve this knowledge. If learners are able to take an active role in this process, they will be more likely to become independent learners, achieving their potential.

Summative assessment

Summative assessment usually occurs at the end of a module or course. It measures the achievement of a learner against the criteria for the module. Feedback from a summative assessment task can help learners to recognise their achievement of the criteria and can lead to future development. Examples of summative assessment are:

- examinations/tests;
- portfolios;
- presentations;
- essays;

- performances;

- artefacts;

- demonstration of a skill.

Feedback for learning

We have explored the important role of assessment for learning, but assessment without feedback is pointless. The purpose of giving feedback is to recognise what the learner has achieved and also to identify development points to help the learner improve their work. To be effective and helpful, feedback needs to be constructive by identifying particular areas of strength and also clear development points, explaining how the performance could be improved. Ideally these should be linked to the learning objectives. Feedback should be provided in a timely manner so that learners can remember what they have done and have time to make improvements before their next assessment.

Feedback needs to be written or explained in such a way that the learner can understand it. It is helpful if you can get them to identify what improvements can be made, but where this is not possible you will need to be very specific yourself. Learners need to be clear about what they can do to improve their performance in future assessments. If you have identified a large number of areas for development, it may be disheartening for a learner if they receive a long list of action points, so you will need to decide what are the most important points that need to be addressed. For adult learners who may have low confidence, negative feedback can be demoralising, so the terminology and tone you use need to be supportive and may involve signposting to other resources or sources of help.

Forms of feedback

Feedback can come in many forms, which will depend on your assessment method. If you have been asking verbal questions in the lesson, your feedback will probably be verbal. You must always acknowledge learners' contributions – it may have taken a lot of courage for them to give you an answer. The learner may have given an excellent response, in which case you can let them know; but if the response is not what you were looking for you will need to ask further questions to elicit the response that you want. Often your feedback will be written if you are looking at work that they have produced. It is important to ensure that your handwriting is clear and identifies what the strengths of the work are and how it can be developed. The learner should be able to use your feedback to develop a plan or strategy for their improvement, so the feedback needs to be constructive and specific to enable the learner to do this. It will also need to be clear how they can apply the feedback to subsequent work. This is discussed in more detail below. There are many ways of providing feedback electronically in order to overcome handwriting issues and to speed up the turnaround time to get feedback to the student. You will need to learn how to use these resources if they are available to you, and also teach your learners how to access the feedback electronically.

Even if it is not given immediately, feedback needs to be prompt and timely so that learners can use your comments in future work. It is useful for learners to know when they can expect to receive your feedback – you may remember anxious times when you were a student waiting for feedback on some work. If they know when to expect it, the waiting may be a little easier.

Feedback on low-quality work

Sometimes you will need to give a learner feedback on work that is of a low standard or is not of a pass standard. When doing so, you should remain objective and refer to the learning outcomes of the assessment task. Explain or indicate to the learner why the work was given the mark it was and why it could not be given a higher mark. It is important to provide specific information and guidance about how they can improve their work in future or for a resubmission. Depending on the nature of the work and the feedback given, it is sometimes better to give learners written feedback along with their mark and allow time for them to read it on their own before discussing it with you. This usually lets them reflect on your comments, enabling them to identify what they need to do to improve their work, and often it leads to a calmer and more focused discussion.

Encouraging learners to use their feedback

For learners to develop their skills they need to be encouraged to identify how they can use the feedback to improve their future work. Therefore, it is imperative that the feedback is written in such a way that, as well as recognising the strengths, it identifies what learners can do to achieve a higher mark or better performance in future. A useful way of doing this is for learners to create a feedback action plan where they identify what they need to do to improve their work, and how they will apply this in their future work. This can be submitted with subsequent work so the tutor can give further comments about how well this has been achieved. It is important to incorporate the strengths in their work too so that they can repeat this in future work. The pro forma below shows an example of a feedback action plan that can encourage learners to engage with their feedback.

Table 4.3 Example of a feedback action plan

Feedback (from tutor)	Development point (identified by learner)	Comments from tutor (in subsequent work)
Spelling and punctuation errors in writing need to be improved	Pay more attention to spelling and punctuation. Allow time to proofread	Only a few errors were observed
You need to be less descriptive and more analytical in your writing	Ensure I explain the implications and consequences of the ideas I describe	A good attempt at this. In some places this has been done very well, but needs a more consistent approach
Show more use of original ideas in your work	Spend more time planning my work to ensure that I have time to use my own ideas and creations	An innovative and unusual approach. You have planned this well

Building confidence and achievement

To build confidence in your learners you should follow the steps identified in this chapter. Firstly, you must recognise that adults have different approaches and attitudes to learning compared to those of children, and they need to be able to identify the direction that their learning will take and the purpose of the activities and assessments they are doing. Courses, modules and lessons must be aligned to ensure that it is clear to the learner what they will achieve, how they will achieve it, the activities they will do and how they will be assessed. This clarity can enable the learner to have confidence in their teachers and the course. Engaging learners in the lessons is key to their participation, so consideration needs to be given to the teaching strategies, room layout and learning experience so that adults are fully engaged and stimulated to learn. Good planning and knowing your learners is part of this. People who are active and participating in their learning will be more likely to enjoy themselves and will feel more confident as a result. We have seen examples of this in the student stories.

The idea of assessment can lead to anxiety in adult learners, particularly if they have recently returned to learning. They may doubt their own abilities and be concerned about their performance. To overcome these concerns, an assessment task may need to be broken down into stages, with a planning phase which enables the teacher to give formative feedback to the learner so they are able to develop and hone their skills. The feedback needs to be constructive and clear so that the learner can engage with and use it effectively.

To build confidence in adult learners their achievements need to be recognised and celebrated so that they can appreciate the progress they have made and build on this further. The aspirations of learners may need to be raised in order that they challenge themselves and achieve the potential they are capable of.

We have talked a lot here about how these strategies can improve the confidence of learners, but planning for learning, aligning learning, using suitable lesson activities and assessment tasks can also help to build the confidence of a teacher. The feeling of knowing that you have delivered a good lesson in which the learners have engaged and achieved the learning objectives is fantastic. It is very rewarding when a learner thanks you for your feedback and you see how they have used it to improve their work.

Critical thinking activity

Identify two recent lessons – a good lesson and what you feel was a bad lesson. Reflect on each of these lessons in relation to the issues in this chapter.

» *How well was the lesson planned? Did it follow that plan?*

» *Did you create an environment for learning?*

» *Were the learners engaged and active?*

» *Did they achieve the objectives?*

» *In the case of the 'bad' lesson, what would you now do differently?*

Chapter reflections

In this chapter we have looked at the importance of planning and designing a lesson as part of a structured programme of learning and how, by understanding how adults learn, we can ensure that the learning experience is planned and delivered in a way to support them. We have explored the purpose of assessment and the role of feedback in this process and the importance of how this builds confidence in learners. These all form part of the teaching and learning process. No aspect of this is more important than another and therefore none of them should be overlooked. It takes practice and commitment to develop the skills needed to teach and support adult learners as well as an ability to reflect on your own practice.

Taking it further

If you would like to explore lesson preparation, teaching and assessment in more detail, you might like to read Geoff Petty's (2004) *Teaching Today* or Susan Wallace's (2011) *Teaching, Tutoring and Training in the Lifelong Learning Sector*.

References

Boud, D (2000) Sustainable Assessment: Re-thinking Assessment for the Learning Society. *Studies in Continuing Education*, 22 (2): 151–67.

Fallows, S and Chandramohan, B (2001) Multiple Approaches to Assessment: Reflections on Use of Tutor, Peer and Self-Assessment. *Teaching in Higher Education*, 6 (2): 230–45.

Harman, K and McDowell, L (2011) Assessment Talk in Design: The Multiple Purposes of Assessment in HE. *Teaching in Higher Education*, 16 (1): 41–52.

Knowles M, Holton E F and Swanson R A (2011) *The Adult Learner: The Definitive Classic in Adult Education and Human Resource Development*. 7th Edition. Oxford: Butterworth-Heinemann.

Petty, G (2004) *Teaching Today: A Practical Guide*. 4th Edition. Cheltenham: Nelson Thornes.

Wallace, S (2011) *Teaching, Tutoring and Training in the Lifelong Learning Sector*. 4th Edition. Exeter: Learning Matters.

5 Using technology with adult learners

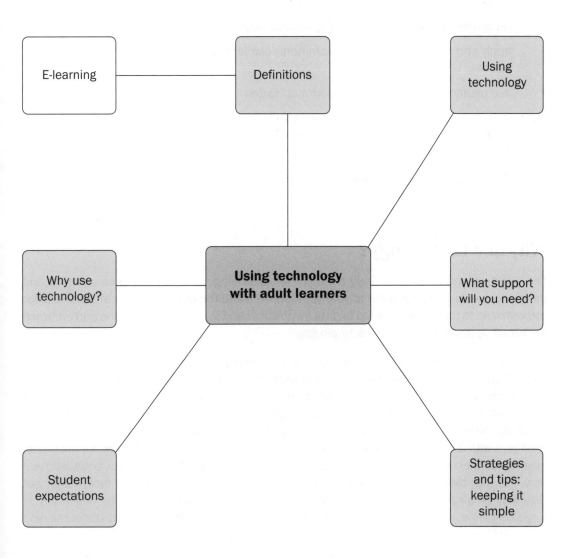

Chapter aims

This chapter explores how technology can be used to enhance your teaching and your learners' experience. We are in a rapidly changing technological world where the use of technology can be a very positive development in supporting adult learning. As a teacher, one of the possible difficulties with this is that you might feel the need to upskill in this field yourself. Or you may worry that keeping up to date with technological changes or developing your skills further can demand a lot of time and energy and could be to the detriment of other areas of your work as a teacher. However, if you recognise the need to embrace and further develop the use of technologies, this chapter will help you.

By the end of the chapter you should be able to:

- feel more confident in your own skills and abilities relating to the use of technology;

- support your learners to use technology in their learning;

- recognise and use virtual learning environments (VLEs);

- apply and use in your teaching commonly available technologies such as mobile phones;

- use technology to aid effective communication.

You may feel anxious about the use of technology and may be at a loss as to where to start. Weller (2007) captures the essence of this possible anxiety when he uses Einstein as an example, telling us that he:

> lost his way to a meeting, telephoned his wife Elsa and asked, 'where am I? And where should I be going?'
>
> (Weller, 2007, p 1)

Why use technology?

The world around us is constantly changing as technological advances become more and more accessible and affordable to you, your learners and the public in general. As a teacher you will need to try and keep as up to date as possible and in doing so recognise and embrace the effective application of the technologies.

Many adult learners have not grown up with technology and may have only limited experience. They will need help and support in understanding its use and how it can help them in their studying. Prensky (2001) describes many adult learners as 'digital immigrants'. By this he means they are new to the use of technology. In contrast he describes younger people as 'digital natives' who have grown up with the use of technology and are more familiar and confident with it. If you refer back to Ben's story you can see an example of how a learner was able to use their existing skills to enhance their own learning effectively. Your adult learners may find that their children or work colleagues have a very good grasp of technology, but they may be afraid to seek help and support from those sources. This can be described as a 'digital divide' and some of your adult learners might need help to cross it. Of course, you may well be a digital native yourself and already have the skills, experience and knowledge to support your learners in their use of technology. It is worth acknowledging that there is an assumption that younger learners are digital natives who will automatically have a high level of IT skills. However, because their use of IT may be limited to gaming, they will not necessarily have transferrable skills and may need as much support to use technology as their mature peers.

Ensminger et al. (2004) identified four characteristics that may help you to understand the needs of your learners:

1. being willing to learn skills or indeed have developed them in the first place;

2. accepting new innovative methods;

3. receiving recognition for using such skills; and

4. having the general resources to use the technology.

These factors need to be considered when engaging adult learners with technology in their learning so that the technology supports them rather than becoming a hindrance.

Critical thinking activity

Think about your own experiences in using technology.

» *Are you a digital native or a digital immigrant?*

» *Have your experiences been positive or difficult? Reflect on what made them so. Consider whether it was the way that you were introduced to them, the access to the equipment, or previous assumptions that were made about your skills.*

» *What role do you think you have in extending your own ICT skills and knowledge and that of your adult learners?*

You may already be aware of the technologies we are referring to, such as interactive whiteboards, hand-held voting systems and overhead projectors. However, you may not be aware of the potential for using things such as tablets, mobile phones and social networking sites in your teaching.

At this stage it is important to note that the educational establishment you are working in will have its own unique set of best practice 'guidelines' and policies. If you introduce new technologies you need to ensure a coordinated approach within the framework of your establishment. You should also consider other factors such as how equipment might be maintained and ensuring that learners are safe. Some of these factors are discussed below.

Definitions

In the field of technology you may find that your adult learners are swamped by the terminology. Each educational establishment will not only have some common terminology, but also some that is specific to it. We will look at some common terms and, as we do so, think about how they are referred to in your establishment.

- **Virtual learning environment (VLE)**: a combination of tools that combine to allow delivery of online content and two-way communication between you and your learners. It can support a number of different teaching approaches. JISC (2000) defines VLEs as *the components in which learners and teachers participate in 'on-line' interactions of various kinds including on-line learning*. It is important to note that this definition may be from a teacher's point of view, but remember that your organisation may well use this platform for other things such as quality management. Other terms you may come across which are forms of VLEs include: learning platform, learning management system (LMS) or managed learning environment (MLE). In addition, your organisation may have its own name for the VLE (eg the X-files) and there are a number of 'brands' such as Moodle.

- **Information technology (IT)**: this usually refers to the actual equipment – for example, the computer, printer or more recently things like tablets and smartphones. It could also include equipment that you might not think of as IT such as digital cameras, dictaphones or the sewing machine that allows you to programme a pattern.

- **Information communication technology (ICT)**: this can best be defined as connecting IT components together. For example, using IT to facilitate communication both within your own educational establishment and beyond.

- **Information learning technology (ILT)**: this can be described as the application of both IT and ICT in a learning context. Depending on how it is used, ILT can be a powerful tool in helping your learners to participate and succeed in their studies.

- **Hardware**: this usually refers to the equipment such as a stand-alone or personal computer, laptop, printer or tablet. It is interesting to note that within this area there is also another set of terminology that some of your adult learners may not be familiar with, such as mouse and memory stick.

- **Software**: this describes the packages or 'instructions' that a computer uses in order to operate. These may include operating systems such as Windows. These tools are important for you and your learners as they enable you to 'talk' to each other. But you do not need to worry too much about this aspect of technology, as your establishment will have trained staff whose job it will be to ensure it all runs smoothly.

- **Programmes**: this describes specific packages designed for particular activities. These may include software packages such as Microsoft Word, Excel and PowerPoint. Most of these are names connected to the specific companies that sell these products. They may also include applications (apps) that are more commonly associated with smartphones and tablets.

In summary, Powell et al.'s (2003) suggestion that ILT is the overarching umbrella which contains (but not exclusively) e-learning, ICT and IT, is a good way of defining this complex area.

E-learning

What do we mean by e-learning? Perhaps it is best viewed as a tool that emphasises and uses ILT as a vehicle for supporting teaching and learning (Hill, 2003). This can be through things like online discussion forums, or access to a range of support materials. By using e-learning in your teaching you may be able to enrich and enhance the content of sessions for your learners.

Weller (2007) suggests that there is a lot of hype specifically with regard to e-learning and that this can be viewed from two different perspectives. E-learning detractors believe it is a way of commodifying education and undermining the professionalism of teachers by replacing them with technology. The second perspective is that of the e-learning enthusiast, who views it as the only tool through which to engage learners in discussion and debate, believing that all learning should be e-learning. However, a more balanced view is expressed by Naace and QCA (2007, p 6) who states that *E-learning is learning that is enhanced through the effective use of new technologies*. This suggests that traditional learning can be improved, but not replaced, by technology.

Using technology

As you become more confident in the use of technology both as a tool for your own teaching and research and as a tool for inclusive pedagogy, you will find there are a number of technologies that are available for you to use. In this section we aim to help you find your way through the technological minefield by examining some of the key technologies. In doing so you will develop your knowledge and understanding, but you will also need to invest some time and energy trying out learning technologies that are unfamiliar to you. You may well find it hard and make mistakes, but don't be afraid to talk to your peers or your educational establishment's IT services, as there will usually be someone who is a step ahead of you and can help you to explore and decide what is right for you and your adult learners.

Table 5.1 sets out the main types of hardware that you may have heard of. We recognise that there are many more but these are the most common in use. As you review this list, consider whether you agree with the advantages and disadvantages we have identified.

Table 5.1 Types of hardware and their uses (continued overleaf)

Technology hardware	Description	Advantages	Disadvantages
Tablet	This is a small mobile computer that uses touch-screen technology and does not have a conventional keyboard. Tablets provide quick access to the internet. The most common brands are the iPad, Kindle Fire and Nexus. Ownership in the UK rose from 2% to 11% between 2011 and 2012 (Ofcom, 2012)	• Small, light and portable • Can be used in sessions, eg for note taking or accessing the internet via a Wi-Fi connection • A growing market of usage and applications	• There may be some issue with the interface between your tablet and your organisation's VLE • Adult learners may have only just got used to using a PC • Cost of purchase: both PC and tablet have similar uses and functions

Technology hardware	Description	Advantages	Disadvantages
PC	Personal computer, eg a desktop PC or a laptop. This is a general purpose computer. It will usually come pre-loaded with software that enables users to create documents and access the internet. It is the piece of technology your adult learners are most likely to own	• Familiarity of use for adult learners • Proven technology • Easier access to sources of help and support	• Large and cumbersome, non-mobile • Need for compatible software
Smartphone	A mobile phone with a touch screen that enables users to make phone calls, surf the internet, instant message and store data, eg music files. Ownership: 33% of 16–24-year-olds, 11% of 35–54-year-olds and only 5% of 55–64-year-olds (Ofcom, 2012)	• Small, light and portable • Can be used in sessions, eg for note-taking or interactive voting • Record sessions rather than note-taking • Can be used to access the internet via a Wi-Fi connection	• Potentially costly on 'pay as you go' contracts • Not everyone will have one • Large volume of apps can be difficult to navigate • May be distracting in lessons

Table 5.2 explores some of the applications that you might find helpful, in particular the use of social networking. This is especially pertinent when trying to develop *communities of practice*, which we discuss in greater detail in Chapter 6. Social networking is the phenomenon of the last few years. Since their introduction, sites such as Facebook, LinkedIn and Friends Reunited have seen huge growth in the number of users. There are over 1.23 billion users worldwide (Facebook, 2013) and an estimated 52 per cent of the population in the UK use social networking sites (eMarketer, 2013). They are web based and allow users to construct a profile of themselves that can be shared with like-minded people or friends. If you are going to use these sites, it is very important that you establish ground rules with your learners and that you set up a work-related space rather than using personal spaces.

Table 5.2 *Types of technology applications and their uses*

Technology applications	Description	Advantages	Disadvantages
Social networking	An internet platform through which users build and engage in a social network. This maybe a friendship group or a group with a common interest. This type of platform allows users to communicate and share information	• Share information • Quick and easy access • Large number of users	• Time-consuming • Can cause misinformation to spread
Facebook	The most recognisable of the social networking sites	• Specific pages can be set up for specific groups of learners with limited access • Support available due to high number of users	• Fear of the unknown • May be thought of as a younger person's activity • May be seen to provide too much personal information (lack of privacy) • Security settings can be difficult to set
Twitter	An online social networking site that allows users to send messages that are up to 140 characters long. These are known as tweets	• Instant and to the point • Can be 'controlled' by the use of hashtags • Can help with collaborative writing in a fun way • Can help to record reflective activities	• Fear of the unknown • Too few characters to make it meaningful • Validity of information is unreliable • Only accessible to those in your network

Table 5.3 explores some of the uses of technology in supporting communication and collaborative working. We think these are important tools in engaging your adult learners. One of the distinct advantages of using technology in this capacity is that it enables learners to be in different locations but still collaborate on their learning.

Table 5.3 Uses of technology to support communication and collaboration

Technology: supporting communication and collaborative working	Description	Advantages	Disadvantages
Skype	A programme that enables the user to interact and communicate with other users by text message, voice and video	• Free to download • Easy to set up an account • Easy to use • Allows learners who live and study in different locations to communicate and collaborate with peers and teachers	• Can be poor-quality sound/picture if internet connection is not good • Can be difficult to find other users if exact Skype name is not known • Needs the Skype partner to be logged on as well • Needs additional hardware such as microphone and headset • You need to agree a time to message and be online
Instant messaging	A form of online chat that is in real time. Messages are typed rather than being spoken	• A good peer support mechanism • Can leave an instant message if recipient logged on • A large number of providers, including your own establishment's VLE • Instant responses • Allows collaboration outside the main study period for learners who live and study in different locations	• New comments and posts to be monitored and validated normally by the teacher • Can be time consuming

Technology: supporting communication and collaborative working	Description	Advantages	Disadvantages
Wiki	A series of web pages which can be added to by users. These may be found on your organisation's own VLE	• Other learners can post comments	• Non-academic, it can be personal
Blog (web log)	An online reflective journal	• Aids reflective thinking • Can be used to enhance tutorial support	• Time for tutor to monitor

Once you have decided which of the technologies you are going to use with your adult learners you will need to consider the detailed application of them. You will need to judge how best to use them and, most importantly, their use in improving the quality of the learning process. It is important that you determine exactly what you want to achieve when using the technologies so that they add something more to the learning experience than mere novelty. Using technology alongside other methods can still be defined as e-learning, which in its widest sense means learning using a variety of media, both traditional and new (Hill, 2003). This is the type of approach that teachers of adults find most useful.

Critical thinking activity

You would like your learners to undertake an assessed piece of work as a group. They all live within a ten-mile radius of your educational establishment, but due to family and work commitments they find it difficult to meet outside the normal session hours.

» *Explain how you might facilitate this activity. You may like to consider things such as encouraging the use of Skype or a discussion board.*

» *Consider what rules you may need to set in this instance.*

» *Also think about whether you want to see the work in progress.*

» *Might you want to encourage use of document-sharing facilities?*

» *What might be the advantages and disadvantages of this?*

What support will you need?

Ebersole and Vorndam's (2003) research found that barriers to the adoption of new educational technologies included lack of time and confidence, together with users' doubts about the benefits of using this technology. However, having the skills and confidence to use the technology, and supporting your learners to develop these, are essential parts of your role as a teacher. We can see this in Nisha's story. She was confident using technology and introduced this to her learners by using online discussion forums, an approach which is particularly useful when working with adult learners.

In order to support your learners you will need to develop two sets of skills: technical and pedagogical. Technical skills are the skills that you will need to manage a VLE, such as uploading files, setting up and maintaining discussion boards, recording lectures, using multimedia, setting up and using online assessments/tests, and using communication tools such as Skype. The pedagogical skills you will need include such things as introducing your adult learners to the VLE for your educational establishment, providing opportunities for them as individuals and as small groups to engage with online materials, and providing opportunities for them to engage in communication outside the classroom in order to share ideas and provide peer feedback. Technical skills can be developed by attending staff development sessions within your own establishment and by using your peers to help you. You know how important peer support is for your learners, but it is equally as important to you in developing your skills and knowledge and in becoming part of a community of practice in your workplace. Nisha, for example, could share her experience with her colleagues as they may wish to include this approach in their teaching too, and she could support them in this.

Student expectations

The following quote is from an adult student on an access to e-learning course.

> *I'm still learning and still don't see myself as a technical person, but I can see how all this [learning technology] makes a difference. That's what motivates me to keep learning.*

(JISC, 2009, p 9)

This illustrates how important the use of technology can be as a learning tool. This section looks at what your learners might expect of you as their teacher. This may include expectations that you will:

- lead them by example: make your sessions interactive and 'showcase' the use of technology where appropriate;

- model good practice by keeping your own skills and knowledge up to date and by using technology to facilitate communication, eg responding in a timely manner to e-mails;

- not use technology as a crutch for poor preparation or indeed to be 'hip and trendy', which can frustrate or distract learners;

- use technology that enables them to fit in their study at times convenient to them (as many of your adult learners lead complex lives with family and work commitments); and

- ensure the resources are relevant and available. Ben's story is a good illustration of this – because of his shift work he wanted to be able to access materials online.

Expectations of you as a teacher may well exceed what your educational establishment expects of you in terms of solving learners' ILT issues. With this in mind, it is important that you clarify early on to a new group of learners issues such as who has access to what types of hardware and software. You may need to suggest to your learners that they purchase certain types of software to support their learning. Check with your IT services as they will often be able to guide learners about how to access software either free over the internet or at a much reduced fee. If you have a learner who does not have internet access at home you will have to consider how you will communicate with them and ensure they have access to the same resources as others. It may be that you give out paper copies of materials or give them time each week when they attend to use the IT facilities in your establishment in order to download what they need.

Critical thinking activity

Imagine that within your group of learners you have two who only have internet access whilst at work and several who do not have up-to-date software.

» *How would you ensure that none of your learners are at a disadvantage?*

» *How would you ensure you continue to provide consistent learning opportunities for all of your learners?*

» *What methods would you use to communicate with the group?*

Strategies and tips: keeping it simple

Here are some practical ideas about how you might use technology. The list is not exhaustive but it should give you some good starting points.

- Think about how you will use technology to remove barriers for your adult learners and thus enable them to either become part of the digital generation or further develop their skills in an educational context. Above all, your learners will need to see you as a teacher using technology effectively. In other words, you need to model good practice. Remember that you should use your peer support network and staff development opportunities to further enhance your own skills and knowledge. You may also find it helpful to practise using technologies such as Skype and social networking sites with your friends and colleagues, so that you can get used to them before you start using them in your teaching.

- Embedding the use of technology from an early stage is a vital aspect of ensuring your adult learners are supported and feel confident and comfortable using it. Think about how you will introduce this. In Chapter 4 we discussed the fact that adult learners need to know the purpose of something before they fully engage with it. The use of tasters/tasks which are non-assessed can be very helpful, but it would be useful to the learners if you explain *why* they are doing them. Such tasks allow you and your learners to 'have a go' at using the VLE and other software packages. It is best if these early forays into technology are not part of a summative assessment. Rather they should be formative and enable all parties to recognise the issues that using technology may raise. You will recall in Hadas' story how her teacher set simple tasks for the group every week – this may be something that you could build into your lessons.

- Set clear expectations from the start. For example, let your learners know what materials there will be from sessions and when they will be available. It may be that you agree that the PowerPoint or other presentations are uploaded onto a VLE the week before, or maybe after the session. You may need to be flexible in this, of course, especially if you have learners who have additional needs such as those with dyslexia, as they will need to access materials in advance. In this particular context it is important that you listen to learners, as they will be able to tell you what works best for them.

- Use technology to help develop a community of practice. Think about encouraging use of social networking sites, but be aware of some of the dangers. A practical example of this may be the use of a Facebook page or a Wiki for learners to use before a course starts. This will help them to begin to develop a community of practice and help the transition into learning, taking away some of the initial fears and concerns that they may have. The use of a page such as this could be continued during subsequent holiday periods.

- Ensure you use technology for communication: using e-mails and applications such as Skype to help your learners engage not only with you but also with each other. However, as with any electronic communication, it is worth considering establishing some ground rules from the outset. These may include things such as how long your learners can expect to wait for a response to e-mails and the need for them to adopt a professional approach to their discussions.

- Your VLE may have a function called 'FAQ', which are frequently asked questions. This can be a very useful resource to develop as you can build up a list of questions with appropriate responses that will form an additional source of information for learners. The learners should then be encouraged to refer to this initially if they have a question about their course, studies or their assignments. You can develop this by copying any questions that you have been asked by the learners, or those that you think they may ask, and including the responses. This can save you a lot of time in the long term as you will not have to answer the same questions repeatedly.

Chapter reflections

This chapter has discussed the range of technologies that are available to you in your teaching. It has examined some of the advantages and disadvantages of using specific types of technology and suggested practical ways in which you can use the technology to enhance your teaching and your learners' engagement with that teaching. You should now be able to reflect on what you feel comfortable using and identify areas where you need to develop your skills further.

Taking it further

If you would like to find out more about this vast and somewhat complex area you may find the following helpful: Gilly Salmon's (2006, 2007) works provide clear and practical support for you in developing your skills. They are listed in the references section below. In addition, the following websites may help you:

www.techforteachers.net/

www.edudemic.com/50-education-technology-tools-every-teacher-should-know-about/

References

Ebersole, S and Vorndam, M (2003) Adoption of Computer Based Instructional Methodologies: A Case Study. *International Journal of e learning*, 2 (2): 15–20.

eMarketer (2013) *Social Networking to Reach Half the UK Population This Year*. Available at: www.emarketer.com/Article/Social-Networking-Reach-Half-UK-Population-This-Year/1010032#iGXFdsQBKzkMosD0.99. Last accessed 13 March 2014.

Ensminger, D, Surry, D, Porter, B and Wright, D (2003) Factors Contributing to the Successful Implementation of Technology Innovations. *Educational Technology and Society*, 7 (3): 61–72.

Facebook (2013) *Key Facts*. Available at: https://newsroom.fb.com/Key-Facts. Last accessed 14 March 2014.

Garrison, D, Anderson, A (2003) *E-Learning in the 21st century: A Framework for Research and Practice*. London: Routledge Falmer.

Giddens A, (2001) *Runaway World: How Globalisation is Shaping our World*. London: Routledge.

Gillespie, G, Boulton, H, Hramiak, A, and Williamson, R (2007) *Learning and Teaching with Virtual Learning Environments*. Exeter: Learning Matters.

Hill, C (2003) *Teaching Using Information and Learning Technology in Further Education*. Exeter: Learning Matters.

JISC (Joint Information Systems Committee) (2000) *Circular 7/00: MLEs in Further Education: Progress Report*. JISC.

JISC (2009) *Effective Practice in a Digital Age*. Bristol: HEFC.

Klopfer, E, Osterweil, S, Groff, J and Haas, J (2009) *Using Technology of Today, in the Classroom Today*. Available at http://education.mit.edu/papers/GamesSimsSocNets_EdArcade.pdf. Last accessed 9 September 2013.

Naace and QCA (2007) *E-learning: What it is, Why it is Important and How it Will Develop*.

Ofcom. *The Communications Market Report*. Available at http://stakeholders.ofcom.org.uk/market-data-research/market-data/communications-market-reports/cmr12/. Last accessed 9 September 2013.

Powell, B, Knight, S and Smith, R (2003) *Managing inspection and ILT*. Coventry: BECTA.

Prenksy, M (2001) Digital Natives, Digital Immigrants. *On the Horizon*, 9 (6): 1–6.

Salmon, G (2007) *E-moderating: the Key to Teaching and Learning Online*. Abingdon: Routledge Falmer.

Salmon, G (2006) *E-tivities: the Key to Active Online Learning*. Abingdon: Routledge Falmer.

Thomas E, and Jollis T (2005) *Literacy for the 21st century: an Overview and Orientation Guide to Media Literacy Education*. Los Angeles: UCLA Centre for Communication Policy.

Weller, M (2007) *Virtual Learning Environments*. Abingdon: Routledge Falmer.

6 Building relationships

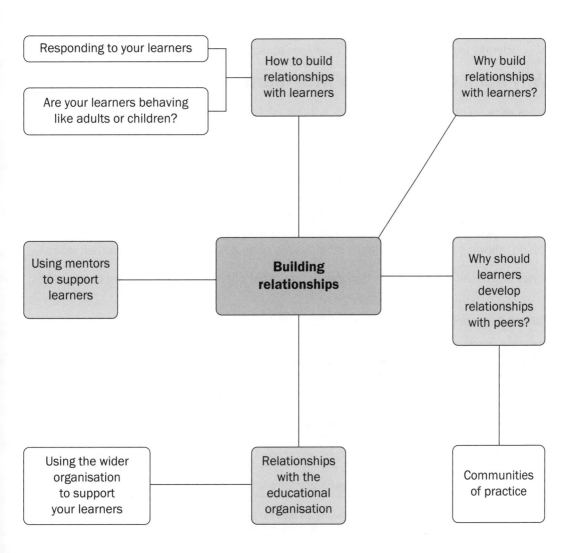

Responding to your learners

Are your learners behaving like adults or children?

How to build relationships with learners

Why build relationships with learners?

Using mentors to support learners

Building relationships

Why should learners develop relationships with peers?

Using the wider organisation to support your learners

Relationships with the educational organisation

Communities of practice

Chapter aims

This chapter explores how you can build relationships with adult learners and how they build relationships with one another and with their educational organisation. This is an important part of supporting your learners on their journey. The text examines why it is necessary to understand your learners, how you can promote a positive rapport with them, and how they can use their peers and a wider support network to help them in their studies.

By the end of the chapter you will be able to:

- identify why it is important to understand your learners;

- suggest ways in which you can build successful relationships with your learners and they can build supportive relationships with their peers;

- analyse the role that you adopt and how that can influence learner behaviour;

- explore the role that the educational organisation and the services it offers has on your learners;

- identify techniques to use wider services to help you support your learners and yourself.

Why build relationships with learners?

In his work on an engagement-based learning and teaching approach (EBLT), Jones (2008) identified that building relationships with learners can increase student motivation, resulting in higher engagement with their academic work. He also states that it is the teacher's role to engage their learners, and that you should not expect the learner to be automatically engaged when they come to class. If we think about adult learners, many of whom have busy days and may well have their minds on other things such as work or family issues, they may not find it easy to switch off from these distractions when they enter the class. Therefore you, as their teacher, have to learn how to motivate and engage learners at the beginning of the lesson, allowing them time to leave other issues behind so they can focus on their lesson.

Jones discusses a relationship framework for school pupils which has a number of phases:

Table 6.1 Relationship framework

Phase	How the pupil feels
Isolation	Isolated from teachers, peers and even parents
Known	Feels known by teachers and peers, but may be little interaction
Receptive	Genuine interest and concern is shown by teachers and peers
Reactive	Support is given by teachers, but feels inconsistent
Proactive	Others are taking an interest in the pupil and providing support

Phase	How the pupil feels
Sustained relationship	Feels part of an ongoing relationship where there is consistent support available
Mutually beneficial	A positive relationship is fully embedded with teachers, pupils and parents

We can relate Jones' ideas equally well to the adult learner who also needs a structure of sustained support through which the teacher demonstrates belief in the learner's abilities, thereby raising their confidence and self-esteem. Think about Ed's story in Chapter 2 and the feelings he started with. He expressed many doubts about his confidence and would have benefited from the quick development of a sustained relationship with his teacher.

A teacher who shows inconsistency in their relationships with learners can sow seeds of doubt into the learners' minds, and if this becomes evident when the learner already has low confidence then it can have a negative impact on motivation and engagement. If you also look at this from the perspective of a teacher, learners can come to your classroom distracted or in a bad mood as a result of various issues that are unrelated to their studies. A teacher who does not know their learners and is unable to understand this behaviour could interpret this as meaning that the learner is not interested in the lesson and is unimpressed with the teacher, which can affect the teacher's confidence and motivation, in turn impacting on the student. We saw how this happened in Debbie's situation and it was detrimental to the learners and her. So, it is important for *both* the learner and the teacher that sustained positive relationships are developed.

In a study that explored the link between teacher support and student engagement and achievement, Klem and Connell (2004) found that students tended to receive more attention and support from teachers when they were engaged in their lessons. However, they did also identify that there were examples where some teachers were able to recognise that less-engaged learners needed more support and therefore deliberately targeted their attention that way. They also found that students who considered that their teachers had created caring and well-structured learning environments with clear, fair expectations were more likely to engage in their studies.

Critical thinking activity

»   *Think about your own learning experiences and consider whether the relationship that you had with your teacher had an impact on your enthusiasm and engagement in your learning. Explain your answer with examples.*

»   *Now think about yourself as a teacher: how engaged are your learners? What role do you have in developing a caring, well-structured learning environment?*

How to build relationships with learners

You have seen why it is important to build good relationships and support with learners, so how can you do this? It is important to start by considering what might motivate your learners to join the course. This is an area we have discussed in detail in Chapter 3. Then consider the purpose of the course that is being studied – is it a vocational course, part of career progression, to learn a particular skill, or to achieve a particular qualification or award? Or is its purpose self-satisfaction or personal interest? By bearing this in mind, you will start to understand who your learners are and why they have enrolled on the course. You then need to find out a bit more about them, such as:

- How far do they have to travel?

- Have they studied before, and if so where and when did they do this?

- Do they attend after a day at work?

- Do they have family responsibilities?

This information can be obtained through a simple icebreaker or introduction activity. You don't need to know the precise personal details for each of your learners, just gain an overall picture of your student cohort. Once you have this information you will be in a better position to interpret some of the body language or emotions that your learners display. Lawrence (2000) identified some key qualities that can enable teachers to develop a culture of acceptance and show genuine care and empathy to learners. These can be explored and applied to adult learners.

- Eye contact: it is important to look at all learners in the class in a natural way. Wherever you can, arrange the seating so that you can see all of the learners, and avoid just looking at a certain group. Be careful not to stare!

- Smile: whenever it is appropriate in the lesson greet the learners with a friendly smile.

- Think about your tone: use a gentle reassuring voice, not a harsh, aggressive one. If learners get aggravated or annoyed, keep calm and reassuring, but be firm. Sometimes learners get annoyed if they don't understand something or the reason for it, so be prepared to explain.

- Give a relaxed appearance: sit, stand or walk about in a relaxed way. Move into the student space when appropriate (without looking over their shoulders) to cut down invisible barriers between you and them.

- Encourage the learners to express their feelings. If you have explained something to them you can ask whether it makes sense. By adding that you are not sure if you explained it clearly, it gives learners an opportunity to ask for clarity in a non-challenging way and puts the onus on you, not them.

- Use opportunities to show that you trust the learners. The level of this trust will depend on who you are teaching, but you need to show that you trust them in order for them to trust you.

- Have empathy with your learners. This is not the same as sympathy, which shows pity or compassion. Empathy demonstrates understanding that recognises the learner's situation and seeks to support them in resolving it. Sometimes, paraphrasing their words and reflecting them back at them can show your understanding and help learners to work towards a resolution.

- Reflecting the learners' feelings can show that you genuinely care, for example by recognising that they are under pressure to complete an assignment and have conflicting demands on their time. You may be able to suggest ways to help them improve their time management and planning to achieve the deadlines.

- Give learners a chance to talk about their own backgrounds and interests. If there is time, a good opportunity to do this is before a lesson, when learners come into class and settle down. If you comment on a nice bag or coat, they might see that as an invitation to talk to you about themselves. Whilst you will not have time for a life story, a short exchange of information can leave them feeling that you genuinely care about them as a person, not just a student. This can help to break down barriers, which is especially important for adult learners whose expectations of education may be different from those of younger learners.

- Show learners that you are interested in them. By expressing your concern that they are often late or agitated you demonstrate that you genuinely care about them and their achievement in their studies.

These techniques can help you to build relationships with your learners to improve their learning experience. The friendly approach that James' teacher had was particularly important to him as he returned to education after being made redundant from his job. Above all, it is very important to be enthusiastic. This may not be easy if you are teaching in an evening after a busy day, but your learners are unlikely to be enthusiastic if you are not.

Responding to your learners

Jones (2008) identifies a number of behaviours that can influence the development of relationships with learners, such as avoiding the use of 'put-downs' and instead using encouraging words and feedback, identifying learners' unique talents and strengths. Through research into the experiences of adult learners, Waller (2006) describes learning as a mature part-time student as a second chance at education for individuals who were unmotivated or low achievers at school. For learners who have experienced this in compulsory education, it is particularly important that feedback is encouraging and supportive; and whilst the weaknesses in their work do need to be identified, these should be made clear and presented in such a way that the learner has the ability to improve them. It is also important to celebrate accomplishments, particularly when the learners are studying a course that extends over a long period of time and the end point may seem a long way off. (We looked in more detail at giving constructive feedback in Chapter 4.) You can be a role model for your learners, especially if you have had similar experiences and challenges yourself. Jones (2008) also discusses the importance of active listening, which shows your learner that you are interested in them and that you care. You can achieve this by making eye contact, listening to what the student is saying and giving a suitable and relevant response. Where you don't have time to engage in a lengthy discussion, you should inform them of this and suggest that you can continue the conversation at a later date, if this is appropriate. If you don't have time to respond in full to an e-mail, it is a good idea to reply briefly to inform your student about when they can expect a more detailed response.

As identified by Swain and Hammond (2011), part-time mature learners often become focused on practicalities of studying and can become frustrated by an apparent lack of information and guidance. You should recognise this and may need to employ different ways of communicating information to them. Avoid giving important information out only at the beginning of a lesson when they may be arriving late or distracted. Similarly, the end of a lesson is not a good time as learners may be rushing off due to childcare or other commitments. You will need to decide the most effective time to give out this sort of information. It may be after an activity or at a suitable point in the lesson when you know you have their attention. You will notice that Andy has been quite insistent about giving important information at the start of the lesson, but then he gets frustrated when he has to repeat it.

Are your learners behaving like adults or children?

Developed in the field of psychotherapy, Eric Berne founded the notion of Transactional Analysis in 1961. He defined three states: stroke theory states, game-playing states and ego states (Barrow, 2007). Of particular relevance to educators and specifically adult learners are the ego states, in which Berne identifies a parent state, child state and adult state.

The parent state occurs when people take charge or nurture others – very much like a parent would do with their child. A teacher may adopt this state when giving instruction, taking charge of a lesson, guiding their learners and giving structure to the learning experience regardless of whether those learners are actually children or adults.

The child state is reminiscent of an experience that a child may have and a person in this state may show nervousness, or be eager to please, or they may become defiant and unwilling to do something. A teacher who is overly controlling could induce a child state in their adult learners. An effective learning relationship cannot be created when the teacher is in the parent state and the learner is in the child state. If the teacher takes on a parent role that creates too much structure it can be restrictive and suffocating for learners. In addition, being overly supportive can create a situation where learners feel unable to make their own decisions and to trust their own judgement, and it is likely that the learners will then operate in a child state. This can result either in conflict developing as the 'child' reacts to the 'parent' or an over-dependence so that the individual is not becoming an autonomous learner capable of making their own decisions about their learning.

You are looking for your adult learners to make decisions and take responsibility for their learning, so you need to aim for yourself and your learners to be operating in Berne's third state – the adult state. You can do this by involving them in their learning, getting their feedback, allowing them to make decisions, inviting them to think and be reflective about their participation and learning, engaging in peer feedback and asking questions. This approach can help to avoid conflict and create a positive and productive learning environment.

Critical thinking activity

» Reflect on your own educational journey. Think about situations that you have experienced as either a teacher or a learner which have been uncomfortable, or where there has been conflict, and consider what state you think you were operating in at the time.

» Go back and look at Debbie's story (page 29). What state do you think she is operating in with regard to her students?

Being aware of this theory of transactional analysis will help you to recognise the impact of the role that you adopt. At the beginning of a course it may be appropriate for you to take on the 'parent' state to reassure your learners who are at a vulnerable stage and very likely to be operating in the 'child' state. However, to become an effective teacher you will need to seek ways to enable your learners and yourself to progress to the 'adult' state by creating learning experiences that encourage them to be reflective and analytical and to participate and take control of their own learning.

Why should learners develop relationships with peers?

One often neglected but important aspect of your learners' experience is that of peer engagement and support. This can be achieved in a number of different ways, some of which are explored here. Some of the student stories have already shown the different ways that peer support has had an impact. It would be useful to look back at the stories about Ed and James to refresh your memory before you continue in this chapter.

What is meant by 'peers' in an educational context? Falchikov (2001) suggests that a peer is someone who has the same social standing and status as someone else. Other phrases such as 'peer engagement', 'communities of practice' and 'professional learning communities' have all been used to suggest what is described here as peer engagement and support.

What is meant by peer support? Piaget (1932) claimed that critical discussion can only take place between peers when those peers are seen as equals. This recognises that relationships with peers are an important part of the learners' engagement and help them to develop their critical thinking skills. The very nature of most education as it exists today means that learners are required to work alongside their peers. As a teacher you will need to facilitate this. Peer support can be used to engage, motivate and help learners in their studies and it is particularly important with adult learners. As has already been suggested above, these groups of learners may attend on a part-time basis, with little time for social interaction, and as a consequence they can find it difficult to develop a supportive peer network. In his story, Ed showed us the impact this can have. Ensuring that the learners are given more 'formal' opportunities to engage in peer support will help them to develop their writing and critical thinking skills and enhance their social interaction, all of which are important aspects of their studies.

Peer support can be viewed in a number of different ways. Tuckman (1965) is probably one of the best-known advocates of group learning. He suggested that there is a link between motivation, achievement and group work/learning.

Communities of practice

Wenger (1998) uses the term 'communities of practice' as a way of describing a theory of learning which recognises that we all belong to a number of different communities – for example at university, at college, at home, in schools, in the workplace and when we engage in our hobbies. In participating in these 'communities' in pursuit of shared enterprises we are part of a community of practice (CoP). These types of CoP can be established in a learning environment and can be very powerful in supporting learners. Wenger goes on to suggest that a CoP has three shared elements, namely: mutual engagement, joint enterprise and shared repertoire. By creating opportunities for your learners to engage in activities that cover those three elements you will be encouraging them to develop their own CoPs and will enable them to flourish on their given courses. Indeed both Wenger (1998) and Stoll and Louis (2007) suggest that by offering learners the opportunity to engage with each other (Stoll and Louis actually use the term 'professional learning community' (PLC)) they will be motivated to find new and better approaches to learning, thus enabling them to achieve more in their studies. CoPs are not only important for learners, but teachers will benefit greatly from the support and collegiality that CoPs can bring in the workplace (Ferguson and Strong, 2010). We have seen a lot of examples in the stories in Chapter 2 where support from colleagues has been a great help to the teachers.

CASE STUDY

There is a group of part-time learners on an access to HE programme. They come from a wide geographical area and are expected to attend one evening a week for three hours throughout the academic year. Most of the group are in employment; they are predominantly female and have ongoing family commitments. Their educational experiences prior to this point have been very diverse. Some have not achieved well at school and have had a poor experience, and others have followed a vocational route since their compulsory education.

This latter group are finding it difficult to write an essay, especially in the expected academic style required of the programme. The teacher is receiving a lot of e-mails with regard to the next assessed piece of work. Learners are asking lots of questions about their writing style, referencing and how they make their work 'read in a more academic way'. The teacher has been observing the group during sessions and has noticed that there is a cluster of learners who appear to have known each other before joining the course. They tend to sit together as a group, whilst the others do not interact very much with anyone else.

Critical thinking activity

Consider the case study. We saw a similar situation in Ed's story (page 25). The need for a CoP in the above scenario is obvious, but how does the teacher create this? Imagine you are the teacher and think about how you would support these learners.

»   *Consider whether you feel that you know who your learners are and what motivates them.*

»   *What activities could you provide to help with academic writing skills? Would they be individual or groups tasks?*

»   *How would you engage with these learners and how would you facilitate their engagement with each other?*

Building communities of practice

Reflecting on the critical thinking activity above, you may consider asking your learners to think about the topic they would like to write about for their next piece of assessed work. Ask them to let you know the general area they are interested in. Once you have all the information, form small groups of learners all of whom are looking to write about a similar topic or theme. You may like to consider using part of a session to share with them how and why you have done this. This will help to keep the process transparent and should help your learners to engage with their group. In this or another session allow these groups time to discuss their topics and encourage them to share ideas, sources of information and contact details. By enabling and facilitating time for your learners to do this you will help them to form a CoP where, as peers, they should be able to sustain and support each other.

Next, consider asking your learners to provide a small written 'proposal' for their next piece of work. You should set a maximum word count. Then ask each learner to gain feedback on the proposal from at least two of their peers. Try and encourage them to use the peers from their groups. You will probably need to help your learners with this activity by giving them a range of exemplars of comments that are both helpful and thoughtful. In this you should recognise the connection with Piaget's work: peer support can be useful when it is provided by 'equals'. However, when the relationship is considered by one or more of the peers to be unequal, it may not be effective, and it may even be detrimental.

In the specific context of Higher Education, and demonstrated in research by the authors (Ferguson and Scruton, 2012), providing adult learners with opportunities to give feedback on each other's work is an important tool in enabling them to develop both their critical and analytical thinking skills and in encouraging them to develop a peer support network or CoP. The type of peer feedback activity discussed in the scenario above is supported by the research of Gibbs (1999) who found that by positively encouraging learners to peer mark a piece of work, four principles could be identified:

•   learners spent more time out of class on problem solving;

•   marking other learners' work was considered to be a rich learning experience;

- feedback was quicker than if the tutor had marked it but was socially amplified, indicating that if the work was low quality and the feedback given by peers was not helpful then they may not respond in a constructive manner;

- peer feedback can hit home more effectively than feedback from a teacher.

Although these principles applied to the specific context of Higher Education, this type of approach can be used with any group of adult learners.

Sustaining a community of practice

One issue you will need to consider is how to help your learners sustain their CoP. Hargreaves (2007) suggests that for a professional learning community to be sustainable it needs to focus and concentrate on what matters to the group members, and establish a relationship that cares for others in a safe environment. You will need to consider providing opportunities for the CoPs to have time together in a structured session, where they can build relationships and agree chosen communication methods. This way you may be able to help sustain the community by adding your voice and support. You may like to ask the groups how you can help them to stay motivated and engaged. The role and function of the CoP will evolve as the needs of its members change, but long-term friendships can grow out of these support groups.

Relationships with the educational organisation

Whilst your personal relationship with your learners is an important aspect of their time as a learner, their relationship with the wider organisation can also have an impact on their enjoyment, development and achievement on their chosen course. Fleming and McKee (2005) suggest that mature learners benefit from structure and facilities that enable their inclusion into the academic community.

The college, university or other educational organisation where you interact with your learners can have an impact on their learning journey. Whilst these organisations should play a part in the learners' journey, it is worth noting that while they provide positive support, they can also be a barrier to that journey. The relationship that the learner has with the 'organisation' can impact on your relationship with them, and indeed it may be something over which you have little or no control.

So what makes an education organisation effective and how might this impact on your learners? Rowe (2003) discusses a number of studies that all indicate the same thing, namely that the 'ethos' and 'culture' of the institution (in his case schools) play an important part in raising the expectations and standards of the learner. In order to achieve this he suggests that there needs to be a high level of professionalism amongst the teaching staff and the institution should have clear polices on a range of matters. He continues to discuss a 'five factor model' of school effectiveness; namely:

1. *purposeful educational leadership;*

2. *challenging teaching and high expectations of learners;*

3.   *involvement and consistency amongst teachers;*

4.   *a supportive and orderly climate;*

5.   *frequent evaluation of student progress.*

(Rowe, 2003, p 17)

Lee et al. (1991) argue that the way an establishment is organised can influence how you teach and this in turn influences your learners' learning. Klem and Connell (2004) suggest that if schools can create a more personalised learning environment, this will impact on learner engagement. They explain this by examining three areas of partnership working:

1.   strengthening relationships between pupils (learners), schools (organisations) and staff;

2.   improving teaching and learning in every classroom; and

3.   allocating budgets to support the previous two areas.

The question for you as the teacher is whether you have any control over these issues. You should focus your energies on the issues that you can control in part or indeed in full. Using the Rowe (2003) model you should take responsibility for providing challenging teaching, being consistent and supportive, and checking your learners' progress. Your organisation can be a help or indeed a hindrance.

Your organisation should provide you with the support to develop your teaching skills and in doing so enable your learners to enjoy and achieve success. Hopefully you will be provided with good leadership that will enable this to happen. Klem and Connell (2004) recognised the importance of the organisation promoting high expectations of the learners, but in doing so they recognised that learners also need support from the people within that environment. This would include you as a teacher and also a wide range of services that the institution provides, such as financial, emotional and academic. These are often, but not exclusively, called student support services.

Using the wider organisation to support your learners

In our experience, a common barrier that adult learners face is the lack of 'open access' to the services provided by the organisation. These services can range from simply being able to access a car park to being able to meet and gain help/support from the relevant specialist within the student support services team. It seems that many organisations provide very good service for traditional full-time learners, but for part-time learners, especially adult learners (who make up a significant proportion of the student population and may attend in the evenings or at weekends), the problem is that these services may only run in normal working hours. This can place a huge burden on you as the teacher as you are the 'face' of your organisation and may be expected to fulfil all of the support roles. It is important that you avoid this situation. Working with adult learners can present you with a range of challenges and you need to ensure that *you* are supported in order to ensure your own physical and emotional well-being. One way to achieve this is to 'practice what you preach' and ensure you are part of a community of practice in your own workplace and make use of the additional support that is available. The tutor stories in Chapter 2 have shown how beneficial this can be.

So what can you do to help your learners? Firstly find out which support services are offered, what services they can provide, where they are based and the times that they might be available. As a starting point you may need to talk to the head of that service about the type of support your learners require. The head of the service will be the person who has the influence and control of the budget in order to facilitate change. Tell them about the needs of the adults you are working with. Describe the help your learners might need. If you take time to explain your learners' needs (giving clear examples wherever possible), you will start to see that the services can be flexible and supportive. Indeed Kasworm (2003) suggests that in order to support adult learners those services need to be run by critically reflective leaders who will push this agenda forward. Consider the following scenario while keeping in mind the points made above.

Critical thinking activity

In a two-week period, three of your learners come to you. All of them have faced significant life-changing events. The first has an elderly parent who needs more care as dementia is really impacting on them and their ability to live independently. The second one has been diagnosed for the second time with cancer, and the third has been told that they will have to reapply for their job and that if successful it will mean a pay cut.

» *What can you do that is within your control?*

» *Identify the support mechanisms that are available to you in your organisation and to your learners.*

» *Can you refer your learners to anyone else? If so who?*

In considering this critical thinking activity you should have covered some of the following ideas. Firstly you would need to make contact with the relevant head of service and seek their advice. At this stage you need to be sure what the organisation can offer in terms of support. There is nothing worse than suggesting to your learner that you can get them help only to find out from the head of service that they can't help. This has the potential to damage your relationship with learners. You should then have a dialogue with your learners about what they might need and where they themselves might look for that help, providing them with relevant contact names and numbers. You will also need to consider the workload and deadlines for these learners and explore how flexible you can be with these in order that the learner can be supported fully. Find out what other procedures are in place which may take into account such mitigating circumstances.

Helpful hint: Why not put together a number of mini case studies to illustrate your learners' needs? Share these with the student services. This can open a very constructive dialogue. In turn you will be much clearer about what you can offer your learners, and student services will have a clearer understanding of the needs of your adult learners, particularly those studying part time. In the long term, in their planning for the future, student services can take greater account of the diverse needs that adult learners bring and as a result provide services to support those needs.

Using mentors to support learners

As outlined in Chapter 1, educational organisations sometimes provide their learners and teachers with support in the guise of mentoring or coaching. There is much discussion as to the difference between these roles. Gravells and Wallace (2007) suggest a definition where a mentor is a trusted friend or guardian and is less prescriptive, enabling the mentee to find the answers for themselves. The name that you or your educational organisation use is not the important factor. Rather it is how that role supports you and the adult learners themselves. It would be worth finding out if your establishment has such a resource that would be valuable for your learners. For some organisations it may be difficult to attract adult learners to take on the role of mentor/coach. It is important to ensure that if your organisation has a service like this the match between mentor and mentee is appropriate. A mature learner may be apprehensive if mentored by a younger student and this relationship might not be considered appropriate. Try and ensure that you know what your organisation offers and if possible discuss with the organiser the needs of adult learners and how they might recruit them to become mentors. Work as a team to try and ensure that you have the right mentors in place. Again this may not be something you can achieve single-handedly, but liaise with the head of service – they cannot help if they do not know what you and your learners require in terms of support.

Chapter reflections

This chapter has discussed a number of issues with regard to creating a framework for an inclusive learning environment. The key thread running through this has been the need to develop and sustain relationships in a number of different contexts. These relationships are between the learner and their teacher, between the learners themselves, between the learner and the organisation, between the teacher and the organisation, and finally between the teacher and their colleagues. We have explored the evolution of these relationships and the impact that they can have on both the learner and the teacher. You should have been able to reflect on your own learning and teaching experiences to understand how relationships have impacted on these.

Taking it further

If you would like to explore in more detail how to build relationships with your learners, you may find it helpful to read *Understanding Barriers to Learning* by Peter Maxted (1999). To explore communities of practice more, you may like to read Wenger's (1998) book *Communities of Practice.*

References

Barrow, G (2007) Transactional Analysis, Pastoral Care and Education. *Pastoral Care in Education*, 25 (1): 21–25.

Delores et al. (1996) *Learning: The Treasure Within – Report to UNESCO of the International Commission on Education for the Twenty First Century*. Paris: UNESCO.

Falchikov, N (2001) *Learning Together: Peer Tutoring in Higher Education*. Abingdon and New York: Routledge Falmer.

Fleming, S and McKee G (2005) The Mature Student Question. *Nurse Education Today*, 25 (3): 230–37.

Ferguson, B, Scruton, J (2012) *Into the Light: The Role of Peer Feedback and Interaction on Academic Skills for Mature Part Time HE Learners*. INTED.

Ferguson, B, Strong, A (2010) Belonging and Collegiality: the College as a Community of Practice, in Wallace, S (ed) *The Lifelong Learning Sector Reflective Reader*. Exeter: Learning Matters.

Gibbs, G (1999) Using Assessment Strategically to Change the Way Learners Learn, in Brown, S and Glasner, E (eds) *Assessment Matters in Higher Education: Choosing and Using Diverse Approaches*. Buckingham Society for Research into Higher Education: Open University Press.

Gravells, J and Wallace, S (2007) *Mentoring in Education*. Exeter: Learning Matters.

Hargreaves, D (2007) in Stoll, L, and Louis, K (eds) *Professional Learning Communities*. Maidenhead: Open University Press.

Jones, R D (2008) *Strengthening Student Engagement*. New York: International Centre for Leadership in Education.

Kasworm, C (2003) Adult Meaning Making in the Undergraduate Classroom. *Adult Education Quarterly*, 56 (1): 3–20.

Klem, A and Connell, J (2004) Relationships Matter: Linking Teacher Support to Student Engagement and Achievement. *Journal of School Health*, 74 (7): 262–73.

Lawrence, D (2000) *Building Self-Esteem with Adult Learners*. London: Paul Chapman Publishing Company.

Lee, V, Dedrick, R, and Smith, J (1991) The Effects of the Social Organisation of Schools on Teachers Efficacy and Satisfaction. *Sociology of Education*, 64: 190–208.

Maxted, P (1999) *Understanding Barriers to Learning*. London Campaign for Learning.

Piaget, J (1932) *The Moral Judgement of the Child*. London: Routledge/KeganPaul.

Pollard, K and Miers, M (2008) From Learners to Professionals: Results of a Longitudinal Study of Attitudes to Pre-qualifying Collaborative Learning and Working in Health and Social Care on the United Kingdom. *Journal of Interprofessional Care*, 22 (4): 399–416.

Rowe, K. (2003) The Importance of Teacher Quality as a Key Determinant of Learners' Experience and Outcomes of Schooling, *Australian Council for Educational Research. Conference paper.* Available at http://research.acer.edu.au/reseach_confernce_2003/3. Last accessed 26 February 2013.

Shaun, A, and Harbour, M (2009) *Coaching Toolkit [electronic resource]: A Practical Guide for Your School*. Los Angeles: Sage.

Stoll, L, and Louis, K (2007) *Professional Learning Communities*. Maidenhead: Open University Press.

Swain, J, and Hammond, C (2011) The Motivations and Outcomes of Studying for Part Time Mature Students in Higher Education. *International Journal of Lifelong Education*, 30 (5): 591–612.

Tuckman, B (1965) Development Sequences in Small Groups. *Psychological Bulletin*, 63: 384–99.

Waller, R (2006) I Don't Feel Like a Student, I Feel Like Me!: the Over-simplification of Mature Learners' Experience(s). *Research in Post-Compulsory Education*, 11 (1): 115–30.

Wenger, E (1998) *Communities of Practice: Learning, Meaning and Identity*. Cambridge: Cambridge University Press.

7 Pulling it all together

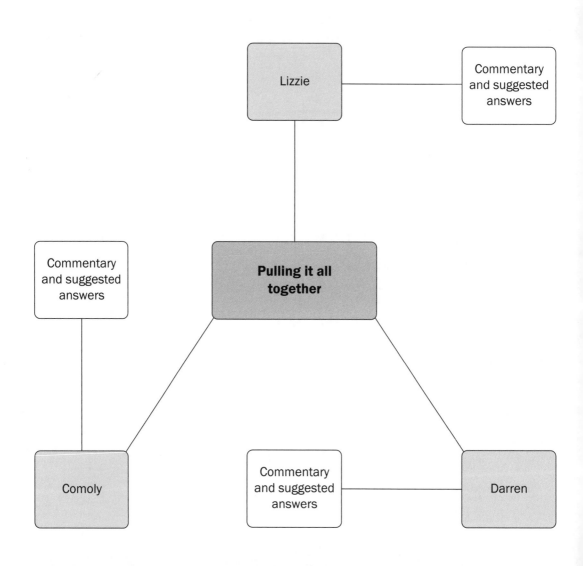

Chapter aims

This section of the book explores some real experiences that tutors have had when teaching adults and it analyses them to understand why the situations have arisen. It considers how they could have been managed differently, reflecting on the issues discussed throughout this book. You will now be able to use your knowledge and understanding of adult learning to analyse and explain these tutor and learner experiences.

By the end of the chapter you will be able to:

*   identify challenges that face teachers and adult learners;

*   suggest suitable strategies to improve the support you can provide for your adult learners;

*   reflect on what you have learned from this book and apply it to real-life scenarios;

*   develop your knowledge of teaching and support strategies for adult learners.

Lizzie

CASE STUDY

Lizzie's story

I started teaching three years ago. I had never planned to be a teacher, I was a manager in a large organisation and I saw an advertisement in the local paper for a teacher in management courses at my local FE college. I decided to find out more and before I knew it I had been assigned a course and was given a timetable. I was still working in a full-time job and then going to college to teach on a professional course for three hours on a Tuesday evening. I was told that I would be supported by a permanent member of staff, and would observe them teaching before I took my first lesson. However, I got a phone call on the Monday afternoon to say that the member of staff was off sick and I would need to do the lesson on my own the following night. I asked what I needed to do, where to go, how many students and so on. I was given some vague responses but I can't say that I was confident at all.

I turned up on the first evening. I had managed to find some training resources that I had used at work before, which I was hoping would be suitable. There were a small number of students gathering outside the room when I got there, but it was locked and I didn't have a key. I had to find someone to unlock the door and show me how to use the equipment. I should have been given a user name and password to log in to the computer, but of course I hadn't. The person who let me in very kindly found a guest log-in for me to use – I have no idea what I would have done without it. By this time the small group of students had grown into quite a large number. Their ages seem to range quite considerably from 19 to 50. Well, I survived the lesson! I decided that I would be honest with the students and tell them that I was not expecting to be on my own and was unprepared but I hoped that they would gain something from the lesson. I wasn't sure what time the lesson finished or if they had a break, so I asked the students what they wanted to do. They were very honest and told me how it normally works.

Since that first night, I have carried on teaching but I find it very difficult teaching in the evening. I don't feel part of a wider team and although I have just completed my teaching qualifications which have helped me to gain a wider understanding of teaching and learning and the post-compulsory education sector, I still feel disconnected from my colleagues. It is quite ironic that I teach management strategies but I am not included in the team by my manager. I know that this is because I am only available in the evenings, but it would be nice if there was some consideration about how I could be included more. It would be really useful to get informal feedback about my teaching and to be able to talk about any difficulties I have encountered. There were simple things that should have been put in place for me – such as how to arrange for photocopying to be done. One learner told me that they had dyslexia and I had no idea what to do. When it came to the assessments, I was really unsure of what happens. I did manage to resolve all of these issues, including a computer log-in, but it took some time and I felt like I was being a nuisance as I had to keep contacting my manager with questions. It was not good to have to say to the student with dyslexia that I would get back to her later, and it took time to find out the relevant information and I needed to speak to learner support and they were not available in the evenings.

I really enjoy teaching and in some ways I feel as though I have been on a journey with my students, particularly in the first few years. I have found the learners to be really engaging and enthusiastic. Like me, they had come to college after a long day at work, so we could share our experiences. I think they respect me for the fact that I am still working in the job that I am preparing them for. Because I was tired from work, I found it was important for the learners to have an activity at the start of the lesson to get them focused. To be honest, I needed it too, to give me some breathing space. I have certainly had difficulties – the delay in getting information to support my learners was hard, and practicalities such as a fire alarm one evening. I should have thought of this and been prepared but I hadn't and did panic when it went off, but common sense kicked in and we were all fine.

The first year of teaching has got to be the worst – you just need to get through it. It takes a long time planning your lessons and resources and working out what level to pitch it at. I had heard that it was a level 3 course that I was teaching, but I didn't know what that meant or how this related to the lessons that I was teaching. I went onto the website of the awarding body to find out and was able to get a lot of information from that. The second and third years have been easier as I knew what to expect and was able to adapt the resources that I had used before.

Lizzie's story is one which is not uncommon for tutors who teach only in the evening. If we look at the positives, she has built a good relationship with her learners. She explained to them that she was a new teacher; her learners respected her as a professional and recognised that there was something they could learn from her.

Critical thinking activity

1. *Refer back to Chapter 6 and identify other ways in which Lizzie may have further built relationships with her learners. When you have done this, reflect on how you might use this knowledge to develop relationships with your own learners.*

   Lizzie talks about feeling isolated from her colleagues. This is one of the difficulties that part-time evening tutors experience.

2. *Refer to Chapter 6 and the section on communities of practice. Suggest why Lizzie would have benefited from having access to her colleagues. Suggest ways in which Lizzie and her manager could overcome this situation. You might find it useful to refer to the technologies discussed in Chapter 5.*

   Lizzie found it difficult to know how to support her learners, especially when one of them informed her that they had a specific learning difficulty.

3. *Using the information in Chapter 6 and the section about building a relationship with the organisation, what do you think could have been done about this and what advice would you give Lizzie about how to manage the situation?*

   Lizzie was unsure of what level 3 meant and how to plan her lessons.

4. *Referring to Chapter 1 and 4, explain what level 3 represents and why this is important in Lizzie's planning of lessons.*

Commentary and suggested answers

1. There are many ways in which Lizzie may have built relationships with her learners. The first thing was that she was honest and told them that she was new to teaching, but she also reinforced her profession so that even though the learners knew she was an inexperienced teacher, they recognised that she was an experienced professional and it is likely that Lizzie brought this into her teaching. As she was arriving straight from work, it is also likely that she shared this with her learners too so that they all felt they were sharing the same difficulties and challenges. The activity that the learners did at the beginning of each lesson probably also gave Lizzie a chance to talk to her learners and get to know them better. If the activities that Lizzie designed incorporated teamwork then the learners would have been building good relationships which will have helped them all through their learning. Lizzie tells us that she had to seek clarification about support for the learner with dyslexia. This shows that she had a genuine concern for the learners and did not just dismiss them but took the time to get a response. This would have demonstrated to the learners that she wanted to support them.

2. Lizzie mentioned that she would have appreciated informal feedback from a colleague and advice on how to deal with certain situations. Lizzie is not part of a community of practice in this role so she is not benefiting from the advantages that this can bring. Being part of a community of practice can help teachers to share experiences, bounce ideas off others and realise that they are not the only ones who

have challenges and difficulties. It is often through informal occasions that this is most effective. Lizzie should talk to her manager about this and see if meetings can be arranged on an evening before Lizzie's lessons so that she can meet the wider team and start to build relationships with them. Lizzie's manager should ensure that she makes regular contact with Lizzie. Technology can be used to facilitate this interaction. For example, Lizzie could talk to her manager and colleagues through a discussion board or a Skype conversation. It would not be difficult to arrange and Lizzie would benefit greatly from this support.

3. The learner support facilities did not seem to be available in the evening for either Lizzie or her learners. Lizzie should have been informed by her manager or by the manager of learner support regarding the support that is available for learners. The organisation should ensure that all learners' needs are accommodated, including those of part-time learners. Lizzie's manager should be liaising with learner support to ensure that this is done. Lizzie could research this information on the college website and also direct the learners to this resource. Lizzie or her manager could also arrange for a representative from learner support to come and talk to all learners about the provision. It would help Lizzie if key contact names and e-mail addresses were given to her when she started.

4. As you have seen in Chapter 1, level 3 is equivalent to A level. Lizzie would need to read the awarding body specifications to ensure that the modules and lessons she teaches are aligned to the learning outcomes stipulated in the specifications. The wording used in these specifications is important as it will give an indication of the level of difficulty at which the learners will be assessed for the award. Lizzie would need to ensure that the lesson objectives and the activities undertaken in her lessons develop learners' skills to build up to this level of ability. The feedback that Lizzie gives should guide learners towards achieving these objectives. The exam board website is an important resource to use as the specifications should be available there as well as additional resources that would be useful to teachers and learners.

Darren

CASE STUDY

Darren's story

I studied film and media at university and have worked for a number of years in the industry. In my career, I was often required to mentor and train young people who came to work with us. I really enjoyed that part of my job so I decided to change career and become a teacher. I am doing a full-time postgraduate certificate in education and have a placement within a college. I am enjoying the course although I like being in placement more than being a student again! When I first went into placement I was really nervous – the staff were welcoming, but it was clear that they were really busy and didn't have much time for me. It took some time to establish a timetable; at first I was just hanging around in the classroom feeling like a spare part, but gradually I started to help the learners with their tasks and the tutor realised that I had some valuable knowledge and experience to share. Although I had a mentor assigned to me, I spent more time with other members of staff as I didn't see my mentor very much. These other staff started to chat to me more about my career and what I had done and it became clear that I had something to offer. In fact it turned out that I had a particular specialism that they didn't, and we agreed that I could plan and deliver my own lessons on this. It wasn't easy to get to know the team as they were either teaching or in meetings, but I persevered and just made myself available and got myself invited to the staff meetings.

I had learned about lesson planning on my course and the importance of setting learning objectives and assessing the learning. I couldn't believe how long it took to plan one lesson – many hours to plan a lesson that was only an hour-and-a-half. I have no idea how full-time tutors manage it. I suppose they are experienced and know what they are doing.

When it came to my first observation, I was really nervous. I knew I had planned the lesson well with lots of activities as I wanted prove to my observer what I could do, but I didn't know how well the students would respond. The lesson was on a Tuesday afternoon and a number of students strolled in late and started to chat to others when they came in. This really put me off and I didn't know how to deal with it. I quite crossly told them to settle down quickly and one of them said something rude to me. I didn't actually hear what was said but it made some other students laugh. I thought, 'This is it, I am going to fail this observation'. I was quite put off after this and was wary that this student was determined to ruin the lesson. In the end it was okay, I ignored the students who were laughing and got them doing the first activity quickly. To my surprise they did it well and enjoyed it. I started to relax and soon forgot that the observer was there. The lesson went quickly in the end. We just managed to do everything that I had planned but it was tight to fit it all in.

The observer's feedback was quite encouraging. He said that I worked very hard in the lesson and seemed very anxious for it to all go perfectly. After the difficult start, I had diffused the situation by moving on and getting the students involved quickly in the lesson. He did suggest that I speak to the students that were late and explain to them about the importance of being punctual and of showing respect for their peers who were on time and for me. He said that I should always start lessons on time so that learning starts straight away so that the students know it is important to attend on time. When I thought about these comments, I reflected that the afternoon lessons do not always start punctually and students have started coming back from lunch late. It made me realise that it wasn't the students' fault that they were late, but it was what had become acceptable; and because I was anxious due to my observation, I reacted sternly which was a surprise to them. My observer also said that whilst my lessons were well planned, it seemed that I was very concerned about keeping to exact timing and did not allow the activities to take the time they needed, so the lesson felt rushed.

At least I passed that observation, but I have another one soon so I need to prepare for that and am determined to prove that I have learned from my previous one.

Critical thinking activity

Darren talks about the difficulty in getting support from his mentor but finding support from others instead. This is sometimes the case in placements where the nominated mentor is too remote from the trainee to provide effective support.

1. *Reflect on Chapter 1 where the role of mentors is discussed briefly. What action could the college take to ensure that suitable mentors are appointed?*

    Darren describes how he spoke sternly to the students who arrived late in the lesson.

2. *Using the information in Chapter 6 about transactional analysis, evaluate whether you think Darren dealt with the situation appropriately.*

    Darren reflects on why the learners arrived at the lesson late. He identified that it was because this had become accepted practice.

3. *Why do you think the observer suggested that learners needed to attend lessons on time? How could Darren change this practice of lessons starting late?*

    Another lesson observation is due to take place shortly.

4. *What advice would you give to Darren to help him prepare for his next observation so he is not as anxious? Use the guidance on lesson planning in Chapter 4 to help you develop your response.*

Commentary and suggested answers

1. Mentors are required for trainee teachers, but the role of the mentor will change over the course of the trainee's experience. At first the mentor will need to be more directive of the trainee, but as the trainee becomes more confident the mentor role will change and become one that supports the trainee in their personal and professional development. In Darren's case, his mentor was too remote from the start and the role was informally undertaken by other colleagues. This is not unusual as personalities and circumstances often dictate how the support is provided. However, the college should ensure that nominated mentors are fully aware of their role and have appropriate time and training to undertake this role effectively, as unsupported trainees will get less out of their teaching practice experience and this will have a knock-on effect on their students' learning. Darren did well to put himself in a position to obtain support from others instead of his mentor and the team benefited from this by using his expertise.

2. Darren has reflected that it had become common practice for the learners to arrive at the lessons late. It must have been a surprise then that he was suddenly cross with them for doing so – a surprise which resulted in one of them reacting to him. If we look at the theory of transactional analysis, it may be argued that when Darren became cross with the learners he was behaving in the 'parent state' and told the

learners off. One learner responded in a 'child state' and made a rude comment. He probably also did this to avoid feeling put down in front of his peers. The good thing is that Darren didn't respond and escalate the situation, and he diffused it by moving on. It is likely that Darren reacted sternly in the first place because he was anxious about his observation. His anxieties are also seen later when he comments that he *was wary that this student was determined to ruin the lesson*. This is an example of a lack of confidence. It is very unlikely that the learner had a desire to ruin the lesson – if so he would probably have found a different way to do so. All Darren had to do was to proceed with the lesson as planned and ignore the incident, and this is what he did. His observer gave good advice though: it was important to speak to the learner outside of the lesson to emphasise the importance of punctuality.

3. It can be very difficult to introduce different rules to an established class that is not your own. This is one of the most difficult things that trainees have to deal with. However, Darren has every reason to explain to learners that in his lessons he has certain rules, and one of those is attendance. He would need to explain this to the class and tell them why he wanted to start on time and seek their agreement in doing so. Of course he will need to use persuasive skills with the learners to convince them why classes should start on time, but getting the students to agree to it makes it easier to reinforce. It is essential that Darren does start each lesson promptly and quickly engages the learners in the lesson so that they have a reason to be there and feel that they could miss out if they are late. He should not expect an instant change in behaviour, but by changing what he does he'll find the learners will respond and may even start to monitor each other's attendance.

4. Lesson observations should be a supportive process, particularly during teacher training. Darren was very anxious to 'prove' to his observer what he could do. Although this is understandable, he needs to relax and use the opportunity to gain feedback on his teaching rather than trying to prove something. If a lesson does not go according to plan when you are observed, don't worry – it happens to everyone at some time. Your observer will be supportive and help you to analyse what happened and how you can learn from it. Darren commented that it was difficult to fit everything into the lesson, and his observer said that the lesson felt rushed and the activities were not given enough time. This is not uncommon in trainee teachers – when you are an expert or very knowledgeable in a subject, it is difficult to realise that it will take learners longer to undertake an activity or to learn a concept as they need to process and understand the information first. Darren did not allow for this in his timing when he planned his lesson and was very concerned about staying on track, so he was not flexible and able to respond to the learners' needs. In his next lesson, Darren needs to be more aware of his learners' progress, and if they need longer to grasp a concept or complete an activity then he must accommodate this and alter his plans. His observer will find this a strength in his teaching rather than a criticism that his lesson did not follow the plan.

Comoly

CASE STUDY

Comoly's story

I studied for my degree part-time whilst working and undertaking other jobs to pay for my course. I really enjoyed studying and being part of a community of learners and am still in contact with many of them to this day. I applied for a job at college to teach on child development courses and I was so surprised when it was offered to me. I never thought I would get the job, but I thought it would be good interview experience. I have been working there for two years now. I cannot believe how I have changed in that time. I feel more prepared for teaching, I think the teaching course I am doing has helped that. The sessions on lesson planning were particularly helpful and enabled me to develop structure in my lessons. I was so scared of being in front of the students when I started, I felt such a fraud. Mind you, I still feel like this sometimes, but talking to my colleagues has helped me realise that everyone feels like that. When I started teaching I was given materials to use and I found it really hard to do. I didn't understand some of the concepts that were in the lessons, so I don't know how the students did. This year I have been creating my own resources, and although this takes quite a lot of time I find it is much easier and I feel more confident about delivering the lessons. I have found, and still do find, the marking difficult. I don't know how much feedback to give. I find I spend ages when I am marking and put loads of comments on the work so that I am probably writing more words than the students are. I am also unsure of how to give a grade for the work; it is not very clear what is a distinction, what is a merit and what constitutes a pass. I think I now know what a fail looks like, but I find it really hard to give useful feedback to help the students improve their work.

On one of the courses many of the students are older than me and although I have experience and qualifications in the subject, they have greater knowledge in some of the aspects that I am supposed to teach them. I don't really understand why they are doing the course as they seem to have a lot of knowledge already. This scares me a bit and I try not to look at these students when they are in my class as I am sure one of them will stand up and challenge me one day. In the early days of teaching I thought this was a real possibility, but now as no one has I think that I must be getting away with it! Although generally the behaviour and engagement is good, the one thing that drives me mad is mobile phones – some of the students are always on them! I have tried some strategies to manage it. One has been a two strikes system – one is a warning to put the phone away and if it appears again then the student has to put it in a box in the front of the room. It can take up a lot of time dealing with this and some students refuse to do this and there is nothing that I can do.

Quite a number of the students have children of their own. Their childcare arrangements mean that they are often late for lessons and I have to repeat the start of the lesson. A number of students also seem to have very little confidence in themselves, which surprises me as they come across very confidently and sometimes I am a bit intimidated by them.

I realise that this is a new career for me and it will take time to gain confidence in what I am doing, but when I reflect back on how I was when I started teaching, I have developed so much. I find aspects of the job really hard, but my colleagues make it look so easy and don't seem to be chasing around like I do.

Critical thinking activity

Comoly explains the difficulty of dealing with mobile phones. This is a common problem in Further and Higher Education as well as in schools. She identifies that she has older students in her class and some have children.

1. *Reflect on Chapter 4 where we looked at creating a learning environment. How appropriate do you feel her strategy is for managing mobile phones? What would you propose as an alternative?*

   Marking assignments and giving feedback is a skill to develop and it is not easy to master, particularly at first. Comoly is finding it a particular challenge.

2. *Using the information in Chapter 4 about giving feedback, and referring to Table 1.1 in Chapter 1 and Table 4.3 in Chapter 4, what advice would you give to Comoly about how she can develop her marking and feedback skills.*

   Comoly says that she feels scared by some of the students because they have more experience than her in some of the subjects. This can happen, particularly when we are teaching adult learners. She says that she is unsure why they are doing the course.

3. *Using your knowledge of motivation in Chapter 3, explain why you think these people might be doing this course. Suggest how you think Comoly can turn this situation to an advantage. How could Comoly improve the confidence of her students? Refer to the discussion about how adults learn and building confidence in Chapter 4.*

   Some of Comoly's students are regularly late for their lessons due to childcare arrangements.

4. *What advice would you give to her to help her manage this situation?*

Commentary and suggested answers

1. The strategy that Comoly is using to deal with mobile phones is not really appropriate for the adult learners in her class. This could be an effective strategy for younger learners, but as we have seen, some of the students in her class have children and may need to be contactable by phone in the event of an emergency. It would not be appropriate to have one rule for some students and another for others. Instead, Comoly would be better agreeing ground rules with the students in the class at the beginning of term and reminding them of these as needed. This would include

getting an agreement about the use (or lack of use) of mobile phones, explaining why they are a distraction so students are 'signed up' to the rule. She would need to talk to the parents in the class about their use of phones. It is important to reinforce the rule, but collecting phones in a box seems rather disruptive and is more likely to make a bigger issue of it, particularly if some students refuse to participate. Comoly is really setting herself up for a difficult situation. It would be better to have a quiet word with the student in the lesson than another conversation outside the lesson. By collecting the phones in, Comoly is treating her students like children rather than as adults, and this seems to be an unsuitable strategy.

2. Comoly needs to establish what the learning outcomes or descriptors are for the different levels of work so that she can be clear what a distinction assignment, a merit and a pass should contain and the depth that would be required. This should be available in the awarding body information. Comoly should ask her colleagues if they have any examples of marked work which would help her to see the level and the amount of feedback that is given. She should base her feedback on the learning outcomes; in this way she can be objective. It is useful to see the terminology used for the level descriptors so that any written comments correspond with this. This would enable alignment in the marking. It is beneficial to have standardisation prior to marking so that the marking team agree what is expected at the different levels. After some assignments have been marked, there should be a moderation process to determine whether markers have been consistent and fair and are marking appropriately. Borderline assignments should be referred to another marker to help with a decision. If Comoly is the only person marking the work, she needs to discuss the marking with an experienced colleague and have her marking moderated. A thorough standardisation and moderation process is not only fairer to the students, it is a very supportive process for the tutors too. To help students use the feedback, Comoly could consider using a feedback action plan such as the one in Table 4.3 in Chapter 4.

3. Comoly is lucky to have people in her class with experience in the subject as she can utilise this to develop knowledge of the topic. In Chapter 4 we looked at how adults learned and saw that adult learners' experiences provide a rich resource – one that we should not be frightened of, but instead should embrace to enrich the learning. Comoly is in a position to facilitate the learning of her students (rather than 'teaching' them) and their experience can be shared, explored and discussed to develop knowledge to a greater level. Sometimes learners do not know the boundaries and may continually talk about their experience, in which case this needs to be managed and the learner may need to be thanked but politely advised that the teacher needs to move the lesson on.

4. Lateness can be a considerable distraction to the teacher and the learners. Comoly should talk to these learners outside of the lesson to find out why they are regularly late for the lesson. It may be linked with childcare arrangements, in which case Comoly should explain the impact that lateness causes and ask them to see if there is any way that they can arrange to be in class on time. This is not an unreasonable request as the college will have expectations that students attend lessons on time. If this is not possible, then Comoly needs to minimise the disturbance that

these students cause. There are a number of strategies that can be used. The students should be asked to enter the classroom quietly and not draw attention to themselves. Seats could be reserved for them near the door to minimise disruption in the lesson. Comoly could consider doing revision tasks at the start of the lesson so the latecomers do not miss new input, or she could give them some detail of what will be at the start of the next lesson prior to it so the students come prepared. Any key information or announcements should not be given at the start of the lesson.

Chapter reflections

These scenarios should have helped you to consolidate the ideas and information presented throughout this book and given you practical ideas as to how you could manage certain situations. Above all, we hope that this has given you reassurance that you are not alone in the challenges you face when teaching and supporting adult learners and that many people have experienced and overcome them before. We suggest that you reflect back on these scenarios as you become more experienced in order to further develop your skills and strategies to provide stimulating, supportive and rewarding experiences for your adult learners.

Index